Quest
for Meaning, Purpose
& Eternity

Andrei Simov Yakimov

ISBN: 1484188888
ISBN-13: 978-1484188880

CONTENTS

PART I
MAN'S NATURE AND BEING

The Purpose of this Inquiry

IS TO:

I. Understand better our world; its composition, structure, functioning, strengths, and weaknesses; so as to enable us to live a life in accordance with its fundamental needs.

II. Better know and understand man, as a human being—in his quest for a meaningful and purposeful life, in harmony with not only his fellow men but also his environment.

III. Study and acquire the needed knowledge and wisdom of the universe so as to enable us to determine its true and complete reality, not only its physical nature but also its probability, viability, and contact with humanlike beings.

IV. Understanding better the mystery of death and man's hope for eternity.

It is imperative that, if we are to make real progress in addressing the above issues, it is necessary that we reorient our priorities and redirect our efforts—the application of our attributes/capacities in a coordinated and systematic method(s) of inquiry(ies), otherwise we'll fail, as we have done so far.

History teaches us that each epoch of human endeavor produces and creates its own mode of attitudes and behavior that reflects its own values, beliefs, and aspirations, which, in turn, determine and reflect its philosophical outlook and convictions. With time and in time, things change, the old is replaced by the new; the new rejects the fundamentals of the old and imposes its own basic core values, beliefs and philosophical views and orientation. This fact makes it impossible for succeeding generations to reach a lasting agreement on the most pressing questions humanity faces today. However, the only constant—that gives us hope—is the quest for the truth that is imbedded in man's nature, which we must never surrender.

MAN: WHO IS HE?
How shall he think of himself?

According to Pico della Mirandola, God said to man: "You alone are not bound, by any restraint, unless you will adopt it by the will which we have given you. I have placed you in the center of the world that you may earthy the easier look about and behold all that is in it. I created you a creature, neither earthy nor heavenly, neither mortal nor immortal, so that you could be your own creator and choose whatever form you may assume for yourself."

Giordano Bruno praises the achievements of Copernicus because he "emancipated our knowledge from the prison house in which, as it were, it saw stars only through small windows."

The English poet A. Charles Swinburne declaims as follows about man:

"The seal of his knowledge is sure, the truth and his spirit are wed,…Glory to Man in the highest! For man is the master of things."

"The fault, dear Brutus, is not in our stars, but in ourselves."

Zeus, in Homer's *Iliad*, states, simply: "There is nothing me thinks, more piteous than a man, of all things that creep and breathe the earth."

In his book *The Nature and Destiny of Man*, Reinhold Niebuhr—Protestant theologian—gives the Christian view of man. He states: "Man is, according to the Biblical view, a created and finite in both body and spirit…

He (Man) is understood primarily from the standpoint of God, rather than the uniqueness of his rational faculties or his relation to nature." He is made in God's image.

…Two facts about man: one, the obvious, is that he is a <u>child of nature</u>, subject to its vicissitudes, compelled by its necessities, driven by its impulses;

…The <u>other</u>, less obvious, is that "<u>man is a spirit</u> who stands <u>outside of nature, life, himself</u>, his <u>reason</u>, and the <u>world</u>." Mr. Niebuhr continues: "God is both vitality and form and the source of all existence. He creates the world. This world is not God; but it is not evil because it is not God. Being God's creation, it is good".… Man, "His essence is free self-determination."

W.S. Kuniczak, in his book *The March*, defines man as follows: "Only through suffering may we ascend to humanity; the passion on Golgotha had made not a God but a man." He defines Hell as "...he saw a soul in Hell, for Hell is a spirit locked up with no place to go, it is time trapped in nothingness between two states of being; its destiny is death."

"The soul that is sinning it, itself will die" (Ezekiel 18:4). Isaac B. Singer, in his book *The Manor*, states: "I believe that every drop of semen contains a spirit, then every man carries within him millions of spirits…latent madness in the human brain always, showed up in a crisis; primeval fears had not vanished. There exists in every one a hidden desire to worship idols, to perform black magic. The Book of Deuteronomy constantly warned against such dark propensities. Whoever its author was, he apparently knew that fatalism was the most profound malady of the soul."

The Hebrew philosopher Maimonides states: "While man cannot know a future event, it is an arrogance of man to assume that God cannot do so; for man's knowledge and God's knowledge are not comparable, God's essence being qualified by attributes not even imaginable by his creatures."

"There is a Divinity that shapes our ends, rough-hew them how we will." Rabbi Akiba states simply that: "Everything is foreseen and yet Man has free will." This for him is a matter of faith rather than of proof.

Regarding the truth, W.S. Kumiczak states, "…The truth of the matter is that besides this joyless, loveless, materialistic interpretation of the universe is another which is above the reasoning intellect and cannot be attained by intellect alone, and in which the universe of matter is merely reflected…"

The eighteenth century German playwright Gotthold Lessing states the nature of truth as follows: "If God were to hold all truth concealed in his right hand, and in his left hand only the steady and diligent drive for Truth, albeit with the proviso that I would always and forever err in the process, and to offer me the choice, I would with all humility take the left hand, and say, "Father, I will take this—the pure Truth is for you alone."

The purpose of these quotations is threefold:

First, the wisdom of each quote is self-evident, so is the manner of its presentation.

Second, the varieties of views regarding the nature of man are staggering, conflicting, and provocative, and yet there exists a common thread in the human mental method of thinking about ourselves.

Third, the conclusions/outcomes implied in these quotes can be unified in a few general categories that define/give identity to what man is!

The two general approaches/methods to discover the truth are:

First, the school of thought that believes that it has found the truth and seeks only to understand and explain it. That is the faith approach.

Second, the school of thought that seeks to discover the truth and thereby understand it. That is the scientific approach.

Each approach has its own subdivisions that in turn make things much more difficult, if not impossible, to reach a common consensus as to the identity of man.

Before we continue with this inquiry, we should first present the required sequences of man's existence:

First, the environment, which will support his existence, must exist in quantity and quality as the first a priori condition.

Second, man is born (created or evolved is not the issue), he exists; he is a fact, a fact that determines his nature—his state of creation, which in turn determines/formulates his major characteristics that define him as a separate and unique creature, endowed with instincts, senses, innate impulses/forces/vitalities, reason, psyche, and spiritos. This is his second a priori condition.

Third, the development and the application of these attributes, that is, his competences, which will, in turn, determine that which makes him be—exist—determines his being. This in effect constitutes his essence—the realization and the fulfillment of his purpose.

This is his third a priori condition.

Fourth, his quest for the fulfillment of his possibilities and capacities establishes his existence as being—being a man!

This is his fourth a priori condition.

Fifth, the last a priori condition is his state of being; the evaluative state—is he realizing his life's purpose?—agony vs. ecstasy; good vs. evil; right vs. wrong; failure vs. success, etc.

Sixth, death—the end of the quest!

Seventh, what next—life after death or the end!

Man is not a single/one-dimensional being, but is a multifaceted, multidimensional complex creation. He is not of matter made but is of flesh, blood, bones, and brains.
Modern man has taken the path that separates and divides him from his nature—perhaps embarrassed by his creatureliness and refusing to be dependent on it and be under its vicissitudes, control, and dictates. He has embarked on creating his own environment, distinct and separate from the natural

one—a man-made, artificial one, building things that are bigger and faster, and he calls this progress! But he is realizing now that the artificial is not warm, nor is it enduring—the old is destroyed so that the new can replace it, a constant change that brings instability, insecurity and uncertainties. The ever-increasing rate of production and consumption of material things causes imbalances to our ecosystems that lead to natural disasters. This man-made habitat misleads man to believe that he is above and in control of nature, and leads him to accept the false premise that he is more than what he is—he sees and defines himself differently, in favor of his newfound pleasures, in his materialistic achievements at the expense of his naturalism, humanism, and psycho-spiritos aspects of his nature.

The Facts About Man

One: Man is a natural creation, so is everything else.

Two: Man is a creature unlike the other creatures/animals. He is unique in his own right—the right of being what he is.

Three: Man is part of and thereby is a universal being; he has a universal purpose, claims a kinship to the creator. He, therefore, can be defined by his inherent attributes and potentialities that correspond to the above facts. The most significant attribute that he possesses is his conscience essence; the ability to not only view himself introspectively—impose a judgment on what he sees, feels, thinks, imagines—but also the ability to transcend his own being and limitations, to step outside into space, behold the wonderment of the infinite, its awesomeness; its creative and destructive powers; forces causing death, new life and the renewal reasserting anew the universal balance and harmony. Man, in this dynamic drama, plays but a small part!

Man's Being
The Four Categories

I: The Natural State of Being:

   A. The physical source—the brain and the inner vital forces.

   B. Description: Are the means to transmit the imbued attributes of being—reflexes, reactions, impulses, alertness; the inner properties to cause action/reaction without deliberate, premeditated plan/design.

   C. The method: To act upon the impulses—to trigger the fail-safe mechanism, to guard and protect the body.

   D. The purpose: survival and procreation.

II: The Senses State of Being

   A. The physical source: the senses as means—via the brain

   B. Description:

      Nose – smell
      Eyes – vision
      Ears – hearing
      Tongue – taste
      Skin – touch/feel
      Muscles – reflexes

   C. The method: the triggering and the application of the body's designated, outer parts—their sensors—to act in unison with the other parts of the body for the benefit/good of the whole.

   D. The purpose: to support, nourish, and protect the body.

III: The Mental State of Being:

    A.   The physical source: the brain

    B.   Description: to think, reason logically; develop language, formulate ideas, conceptualize, establish methods/processes for scientific analysis. Apply his intelligence in the design development, application, and control of his own needs and those of his fellow man.

    C.   The method: to adopt and apply a neutral process of intelligence and reason in pursuit of knowledge.

    D.   The purpose: to seek, pursue, and establish the truth.

IV: The Psycho-Spirit State of Being

	The Psyche	**The Spirit**
A. Physical Source	The brain as fountain	The brain as impulses
B. Description	Feelings: love vs. hate Emotions: joy vs. anguish Consciousness: right vs. wrong, etc.	The will: infusion of power and restraint Conscience: morality, good vs. evil introspection; transcendence; Intuition: imagination, etc.
C. The Method:	Conscious/subconscious bursts and eruptions of feelings and emotions	Shooting of mental impulses: as the sun's rays, through the finite and infinite realms
D. The Purpose:	Establish psychic stability and balance between euphoria and despondence.	Allows man a glimpse into and a feel of the mysterious unknown.

In Summary:

From all of the above, we can say that man derives a state of awareness, freedom, wisdom, creativeness/romance, and appreciation of his essence

on earth and far beyond its confines; a place of timeless beauty, wonderment, and joy—the creator gave us not only life but the ability to penetrate
what might be beyond and after life.

The Major Views of Man's and the Universal Reality: Theories/Doctrines

I.   The Natural Deterministic Approach:
     A. Naturalism
     B. Realism
     C. Materialism

II. Humanistic Deterministic Views:

     A. Inner/Vital Forces and Attributes
         1. Sensationalism
         2. Vitalism

     B. Mind/Reason/Intellect Approach
         1. Idealism
         2. Rationalism
         3. Nominalism

     C. Romanticism

III. Divine—Design Deterministic View

IV. A. Revelationistic Creationism
     B. Spiritualism
     C. Teleological View

Each of these theories/doctrines sees and views man from a different point of
view: the physical, the mental, the psyche, and the spiritual, emphasizing the
proponent's discovery as the one that represents the true understanding of man
and his reality.

Now, we'll examine briefly each theory/doctrine with a brief critical commentary. At the end, I will attempt to construct a general synthesis, bringing together a new view of man and his reality.

I. A.   Nature as Determining Force

The central thesis here is that all living things are created by our respective natural environments. We are all determined by nature. Nature creates all. It maintains that if we see things objectively, dispassionately, applying the scientific method, we cannot but be convinced beyond any doubt that only nature is the determining force that explains fully man's reality. And as creatures of our natural environment, its dynamic forces shape, mold and reshape our human existence—our being. Our dependence on our nature for our existence determines not only our relationship with her but also our relationships with each other as human beings, individually as well as collectively.

It imposes on us objectivism in our value system—our perceptions, feelings and emotions, and morals; everything is factual and, therefore, measurable, value judgment and idealization are not applicable, things are depicted, portrayed in their real form and setting. It also holds that our religious beliefs are a direct function of and derived from the natural world. In short, this theoretical viewpoint holds that nature creates life, nourishes life and destroys life. The theory, in trying to explain man's reality, confuses the roles of nature as a creator of life and as a sustainer of life. The natural environment as a sustainer of life is an a priori condition for the existence of that life, but this fact does not necessarily lead to the proposition that it is a creator of life. It leaves man's attributes, potentialities, and capacities as irrelevant; and it claims an impossibility that they are matters created and controlled; from matter we get force when in motion—but not ideas, feelings, etc. It keeps and holds man too close to the ground, as the animals are, and does not allow him to venture out in space into his inner self to transcend and feel the unknown universe.

Its shortsightedness fails/refuses to recognize that man's progress, his emotional state, and his essence are a function of his ability to reason, his psyche, and willpower—they are real and vital to his existence and are by their very nature normative concepts.

I. B.   Realism as a Doctrine

Claims that material objects, in their abstract/universal terms, do exist. This existence, as reality, is apart—not connected to—how we see, perceive, feel, or are conscious of them. Their reality is independent of how we view them. They are there regardless of man's existence. In short, man does not determine reality.

Nobody argues whether man determines or does not determine reality. The purpose of the inquiry is for man to learn and understand what reality is by the application of our mental-reasoning powers at our disposal. If we do not use and rely on our attributes, how, then, did the proponents of realism arrive at their conclusions about reality that realism represents?

All realities that we perceive, see, feel, etc., are a function of our natural and acquired attributes and experiences; this may or may not be in total agreement with the external intelligent point of view; perhaps someday we'll know their views, but for now this is our reality of knowing.

I. C.   Materialism as a Theory of Reality

Materialism is the extreme of the naturalist theories, and, of course, is based on Marx's dialectic materialism. It holds that matter is the true reality, and everything else is derived from matter and thereby explained in terms of matter. Its view, simply stated, is "that motion and change are the essence of reality, and that general laws of the continual transformation of reality can be scientifically determined; struggles among things is inevitable due to their motion, which in turn causes contradictions between and among the things."

Life, Marx claims, is a series of contradictions, a negation of negation—present in both things and processes. These continuous conflicts evolve, with time, into a cause-effect series of conflicts that will result in new realities—synthesis. Anything and everything can be explained by this dialectic formula: thesis carries its own antithesis, a struggle is inevitable and must be resolved into a new reality, the synthesis.

As matter moves, there will be change if the cause-effect sequence begins to work, but for the whole process to kick in, a spark is needed, i.e., the first cause; Marx does not have one. Moreover, not all matter(s) are destined to/and into conflicts, they move in a prescribed/preordained patterns and in harmony with other matters.

The collapse of the Soviet Union shows beyond any doubt the profound disappointment in the utter failure of the dialectics and the fallacy of its ideological dogma—Scientific Determinism. The tragedy is not only in terms of human losses and sacrifices, which are great by any measure, but also the loss of faith and belief in the author himself by the very people that he intended to free! Those that saw its weaknesses, wickedness, and falseness were silenced by the masses. The most perceptive of them was Soren Kierkegaard, a Danish philosopher whose warning is very clear, according to Malcom Muggeridge: He "fully scorn dismissed such collectivist hopes (referring to Marx's Socialist Utopia), for mankind as infallibly leading to a new and more comprehensive form of servitude. The divine right of kings had been abolished, but the divine right of the people that had replaced it would prove an even worse deception, and would give rise to regimes that exceeded any hitherto known, in their brutality and claims to omniscience. I am the people, Le people, c'est moi, was an ever more insanely arrogant claim than the famous one of Louis XIV's, l'etat, c'est moi, I am the state."

On the question of how to save the age, Kierkegaard asserts the following:

"It is very doubtful, then, that the age will be saved through the notion of social organization, of association (which at best have validity with respect only to material interests)…is an evasion, a dissipation, an illusion, whose dialectic is (that) as it strengthens individuals, so, it weakens them. It strengthens by numbers, solidarity, but from the ethical point of view, this is a weakening. Not until the single individual has established an ethical stance in despite of the whole world, not until then can there be any question of genuinely uniting. Otherwise, it gets to be a union of people who separately are weak; a union as unbeautiful and depraved as a child-marriage."

A matter, if acted upon, may cause a motion and this motion, in turn, may cause a change; but this dialectic process does not determine man and his historical evolvement of his being, much less his origin. Man is not a matter, he is flesh, blood and bones—all in one living creature, with emotions, ideas, thoughts, reason, imagination, and beliefs that provide him with impulses, drive, and willpower to plan and act. Human behavior is a relationship of challenge/response series of events that we, as individuals, have to deal with and overcome. They are unlike those of the predictable, cause-effect outcomes; they are unpredictable and unknown—their outcome(s) is unknown in advance. Their uncertain outcome(s) is what makes life interesting and challenging; it forces us, as human beings, to use/apply our fallible and precise attributes to deal with life's seemingly unending challenges.

The laws of nature, as determined by the scientific method, do not change; they are permanent, as the dialectic process will determine the state of communism—a state of perfect Utopia. But herein lies the dilemma: first, perfection is not an achievable state; it is a goal that we aspire to, continuously move toward, but we never get there. The essence of life is to journey through it. Second, perfection is a contradiction to the fundamental dialectics proposition that motion causes change, and change leads/determines new reality; but this infallible scientific determinism stops once perfection/communism is achieved. Why? Third, perhaps the most naïve proposition ever offered, is the method and the means by which the communism Utopia will be brought about; simply remove the private ownership of the means of production and put them under the state-collective ownership, whereby their control will fall in the hands of the proletariat—the new social class—that is it, simple! But even more amazing is what happens after communism is realized.

I quote: "It, signifying, at last, the triumph of the Laws of Social Activity over hereto the dominant Laws of Nature. Mankind is free, at last, the proletariat is its liberator, people of the world live a life of material sufficiency, free mental and physical development for everyone, in a classless "state" which (in time) withers away."

It is amazing how Marx manages to manipulate and use to his purposes the two laws: The laws of nature—the dialectics, which will bring about the communist state, the Socialist utopia; and the laws of social activity, realized by the proletariat class, will in fact triumph over the hereto dominant laws of nature—his worker triumphs over his dialectics, an irony indeed!

Now, we turn to the next categories of ISMs—the humanistic determinism of man and his universe. These are divided into two major groups: The first, the A group, deals with man's inner vital forces and attributes forming/constituting the basis of his reality—they are: sensationalism and vitalism. The second, the B group, deals and is based on man's intellect, as the basis of his reality; they are, idealism, rationalism, and nominalism. Romanticism does not belong here altogether, but it belongs much less anywhere else.

II. A.   1. Sensationalism

Is a theory that is based on our senses—sight, smell, touch, taste, hearing. It is through them that we become aware of ourselves; our sensory perceptions; stimulation of our emotions and our consciousness; the brain serves as the activating mechanism.

Represented and seen in this way, it places man one step above the instinct-determined creatures—the animals; a distinction of degree not of kind, insufficient to fully explain man's nature and clearly identify his uniqueness. Nonetheless, it is an important aspect of man and his state of being.

II. A.   2. Vitalism:

Here, man is totally seen as a living organism, determined, sustained, and evolving by his inner vital forces, energy, and willpower.

This view of man is like that of the creationists, only seen upside down; its life source is within man himself, whereas in the faith-based view, the life source comes from an outside, supernatural—divine power—a universal in scope.

We are born with it; it is not a soul but acts like one. Its location, like that of the soul, is uncertain. It is an inner vitality that gives us the will to live, no matter the adversities, dangers, pain, fear, despair, agonies, and anguish we may encounter/experience; this will to exist is a common and constant characteristic to and for all men. All men, therefore, are aware of their own existence and the things around them. If I am conscious of my own reality, then I must be! This I derive by the process of reason, but just thinking it does not make it so; it is so because of my experience of being. This vital force is there by the will of the creation of life and is passed on to each one of us by our parental conception.

II.   Mind Deterministic Views

II. B.   1. Idealism

Very simply, it holds that objects that we perceive are in fact our mental ideas or images of them, and are not the objects themselves. It is the mind that determines reality. Certainly, we know things through our mind, instinct, senses, psyche, perceptions, introspection, imagination, and so on that emanate from them, and that is what we perceive their reality to be. We have no other means of knowing; if this is not sufficient, then we cannot know nor understand anything. Viewed from different realms, our perceived reality will, most likely, be viewed differently. This should not, however, interfere with our view(s) of our reality, because it serves our own purpose(s).

The difficulty here is that the mind, in this case, serves as a tool; it sees, observes, takes an impression of an object, e.g., the Grand Canyon—its awesomeness, a natural wonder, but it does not explain its overwhelming power as the naturalists do to impress on you its deterministic capacity. A few examples that may clarify the difficulty here: the use of images in religions—the iconoclasm debate; what in fact is the reality of an icon? Is it a true depiction/representation of a religious sacred/divine entity? If so, should it be worshipped and held sacred, as would be the actual saint/divinity or is it simply an image of these sacred personages created by man in his own mind?

This controversy split Eastern Christianity in two: those who rejected their use, as being superstition, won the first round; but Empress Irene restored the images. The second council of Nicaea rejected iconoclasm and decreed that images ought to be venerated but not worshipped. This example illustrates the fact that since we are not likely to meet, and it is doubtful that anybody has met, God face-to-face, we are forced to seek His reality, the second-best way we can, which is via the images of the mind. We all know that God, the creator of the infinite universe, is not in essence the old wise man with a long beard; but we do it to reassure ourselves that such a God will be sympathetic to us because he is like us and, therefore, one of us; the familiar reduces the fear of the unknown!

Another example is where the mind helps us develop tools/standards to help us understand the reality around us by simplifying the way we see the reality by the use of the abstract-uniform standards. Economic activity, viewed in the aggregate, consists of two sectors; the real sector reflects the amount of goods and services that we produce in a given year at the current market price; its total money value is equal to the quantity of goods and services times the price of each (PQ). The money sector consists of the quantity of money that we need times its turnover, its velocity to buy all of these goods and services (MV). If we are to sell all of these goods and services, the required equilibrium condition is when the two sectors are equal, i.e., $MV=PQ$. Now, where/what is the economic reality here? Of course, it is the real goods and services that we produce and/or provide: the number of houses we build; the number of cars we build; the number of schools, hospitals we build, the number of students we educate; the number of patients we take care of; the number of oranges we grow; and on and on, an endless array of things.

In order to make some sense of these endless things, we have invented a common standard that all of them can be represented in and accounted for—the money standard. We simply add the money value of all the goods and services sold at their market prices and derive our gross domestic product—GDP; we use this figure in a variety of ways to help us determine how we are doing on a quarterly/yearly basis and compare our economic well-being with other countries, etc. Here, the mind has devised a tool that does not directly target the economic reality but indirectly and does a pretty good job of it—it serves the purpose!

II. B.   2. Rationalism

In simple terms, knowledge is a function only through reason, and pure reason is the basis of truth, including religious faith. It rejects theories that rely on the senses, the supernatural and vitalism.

Certainly, man has a brain, which enables him to think and out of that thinking process, he is able to arrange his thoughts, ideas, etc., in an orderly, meaningful manner—logical patterns called reasoning; and when guided by the scientific method of inquiry, the acquired knowledge is quite reliable, but this reliability is limited in time, in scope, and in subject matter; whatever one scientist discovered yesterday, another shall reject it tomorrow, and another shall replace it with a more advanced discovery after that. However, it does the best in dealing with the how questions, but it is not so good in dealing with questions of why and what-for questions that deal with man's inner vitality, his psyche, his spirituality, etc., questions of qualitative/subjective nature; such as man's conscience, his will, perceptiveness, intuition, instincts, introspection, transcendency, spirit, etc.

These are questions and concerns that depend on our wisdom, not knowledge, for their resolutions. Modern man is in awe with his own scientific and technological success, creating an artificial habitat that is in conflict with nature, our natural habitat. Nature endures. Man's creations do not!

B.   3. Nominalism

Doctrine that asserts that universals/abstract things exist in name only and are not real or actual, opposite to the realism theory, which maintains universals or general ideas have objective/real existence.

The assertion that behind my name there is no man is a naïve and disturbing one. It is nihilistic in its essence in view of our scientific proof not only of the existence of our own solar system but "more than 370 planets outside our Solar System have already been discovered....316 stars are confirmed to host one or more planets," according to Dr. Timothy Ferris in *National Geographic* (December 2009, pp.78-93). This tells us that there is matter; matter in motion gives us energy; if there are stars and planets, there must be a design and universal Laws; and if there is a universal design/order, there must be a purpose, etc. Because of this, man feels the need to establish his place/role in that universal order of things. It is his Nature to penetrate the unknown!

II. C.   1. Romanticism:

It is not a theory/doctrine about man's reality but a statement on his condition—of his being. Man's existence is not what it ought to be; it is too naturalistic—defined as being a product of Nature; pursuing materialistic ends, the maximization of his utility by consuming goods and services feeding and justifying his primitive egocentric tendency and inclination, glorifying his ever-increasing greed to a position of success and progress. The romantics saw it differently, as an existence that left man cold, unfeeling, regimented, and constrained; a life without freedom of form and spirit.

As R. Waldo Emerson puts it, he—the Romantic Movement—
wanted to lift men above their ordinary preoccupations into an
idealistic (or transcendental) world of beauty, truth, and goodness.
Freeing men to create freely and express their own individuality
and spirit. "It is a spirit of nature and man in it—its warmth, colour
and spirit. The unfolding of world spirit is its view of history and
see man as being of unfathomable depth and eternal yearning."

In short, Romanticism sees interconnectedness of all things,
nature and man, unified into one harmonious whole, transcending into the universal spirit. It is unfortunate that such sensitive
and noble idealism/movement did not formulate its own doctrine
of man's reality, since it comes closest to placing man and nature
in unity and harmony, where man not only ensures his existence
without destroying his environment but also keeps man in close
communion with the universal spirit that raises him up into the
heavens, separating him from the animalistic state of being. In this
way, it succeeds in defining man as a natural as well as a universal
being, satisfying and in harmony with both of his natures—the
natural and the spiritual.

III.   Divine Design Determinism

It is the oldest and the simplest proposition, that everything including man was created by a supernatural, divine power called God! The
world's major religions believe in one God—monotheism. A God
characterized as: omnipotent—an all powerful, omnific-creator; omni-
scient, has an infinite knowledge/wisdom; omnipresence—is everywhere; infinite and eternal. This knowledge of God and what He is
comes to us through his disclosure/manifestation of His being to man,
referred to as Revelationism. We exist because He willed it to be so;
the true believer believes this unquestionably and absolutely; believers
view man from God's point of view: man is predestined/preordained,
a perfectly deterministic point of view. It is probably safe to say that all
people past and present, with the exception of a few scientists, believe
in a supernatural being. Faith is as old as mankind is!

The basis for man's religious faith is fourfold:

First, fear of danger; fear of pain/suffering and fear of dying—fear of death.

Second, death, however, has a finality that man cannot accept—nor should he accept it as finality; therefore, he seeks continuity to his own being. This need for eternity causes/propels him to explore the viability of the existence of the eternal and the divine; whereby, through worship, prayer, loyalty, and propitiation; he may secure protection, security, happiness, etc., but above all, his God will bless him with a place in heaven— after his death on earth, ensuring his being forever!

Third, man cannot allow himself to think that he is alone in this ever-expanding universe; its enormous size and unknown reality overwhelms him; its silence frightens him and makes him feel alone and hopeless. All these he cannot bear; he needs to know; to penetrate the hidden, the unknown.

Fourth, man, by nature, needs to belong and belong to something bigger than himself; to do that he must find his place in the universal chain of realities; in order to determine his role and thus his belonging in that reality. This religious journey will give man a purpose to live— to be—not only here on earth; but to be also a universal being.

The key to our common fate and different faiths is for us to determine the purpose for our creation and existence. This will remove the bedevilment of the soul that God put in us—the time of its occurrence, its location, and its function(s)—still debatable and uncertain. The same uncertainty applies to the other God's gift, the free will; it, more than anything else, gives us no rest in understanding its nature, purpose, and the consequences of its misuse. The religions insistence to define man as an animalistic and disobedient sinner is repressive and diminishes our other human traits/attributes that are of significance in determining his character and personality. On the other hand, they tell us that we are God's special creation, He loves us, and He will take us to heaven, where we'll live forever. Two contradictory positions that make it impossible for us to believe what is the truth. However, one thing is for certain; whatever God creates is part of His divine design, and man cannot question His will—this is the foundation of all faiths!

Given this—the first cause—then the question arises: Who and how do we determine the true nature of God and His will? The answer to this depends on what man wants. One thing he does not want is to run into nothingness after his death. The thing that he is looking for is the continuity of his conscious being, preferably in heaven; the major religions promise that. The Judeo-Christian-Islamic faiths offer heaven; the Eastern/Buddhism religions offer nirvana. The two approaches to eternal salvation differ in substance and method. The Western (Jerusalem-based) faiths are concerned more with the salvation of man's soul and the way to the eternal life; how to get to and in God's house—a place of great beauty, peace, happiness, etc., the ultimate existence in serenity and joy! The three faiths disagree on the means of getting there, each having its own prophet/messiah that will lead them to the promised eternal place.

The Eastern faiths are more concerned with and are in search of spiritual purity, attainable through knowledge/wisdom, forgoing all human desires and passions in order to connect and unify the individual spirit with the supreme universal spirit. To live in a state of nirvana—a state of perfect blessedness, peace, and bliss. The fundamental difference in the two states of eternity is that heaven is full of/with the ultimate beings, whereas nirvana is filled with the ultimate spirit. However, the characterizations of the two realities are very much identical; both claim eternal existence of peace, bliss, happiness, great beauty, and so on!

The Relationship Between the Four Views of Man

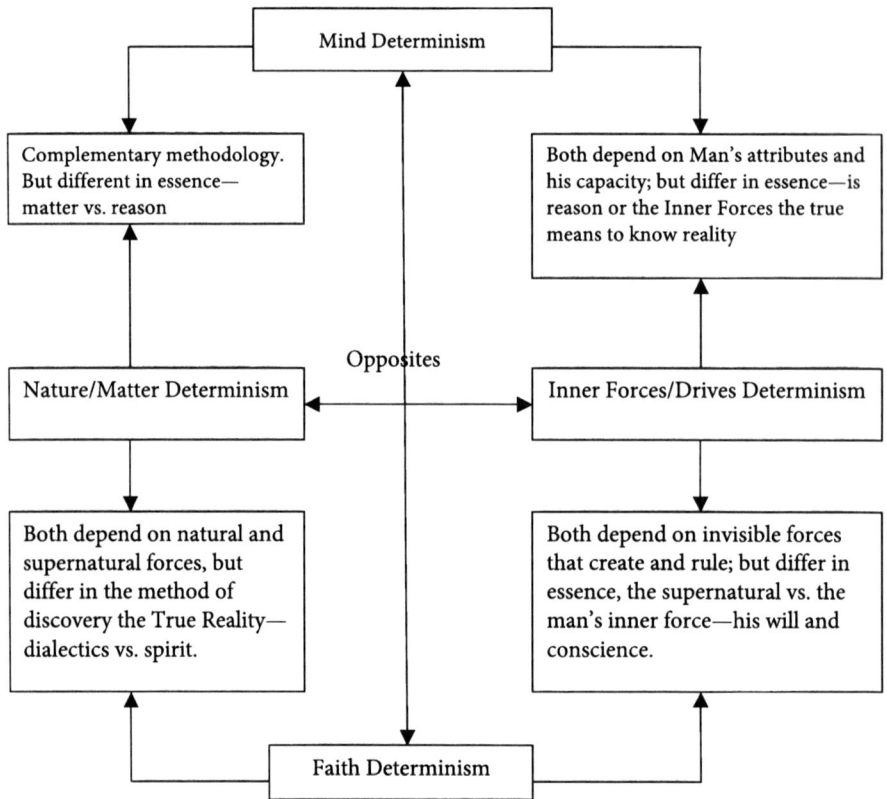

The Nature of Jesus Christ

The Gospel according to John tells us that John, as the witness, tells us repeatedly what Jesus says. And it is these sayings and other relevant information that point conclusively that Jesus cannot be a divinity, on par with God.

Jesus states: "I have come down from Heaven, not to do my own will, but the will of Him, who sent me"—verse 38. He defends himself against the accusations that he infers equality with God, by saying: "My Father." He states—"In truth, in very truth I tell you, the son can do nothing by himself; he does only what he sees the Father doing" (5:19). For as the Father has life-giving power in himself, so has the son, by the Father's gift (5:26). Here it is clear that Jesus is under the direction and instruction of God—the Father: to be his emissary and mediate between Himself and man. To ensure success of his mission, God gives Jesus the necessary powers and needed instructions for the mission; which, according to St. Paul, in his first letter to Timothy, is simply for Jesus to ensure "that All men should find salvation and come to know the truth" (2:5). The strategy is two-pronged: first, perform the miracles, establish legitimacy, trust, and conviction. Second, announce yourself as the true messiah. Jesus says to the Samaritan woman at Jacob's well, after she said that "I know that Messiah is coming and when he comes he will tell us everything," "I am he, I who am speaking to you now" (John, 4:25-26). Jesus did this after he received the Holy Spirit, with which to baptize the converted with water and spirit to create the new spirit-man. All this represents that a warm and trusting relationship existed between God and Jesus; and nowhere does either Jesus or God refer to Jesus as God, having/being of the same substance as that of God.

St. Peter addresses Jesus as Lord after Jesus asks his disciples if they also want to leave him; St. Peter answers, "Lord, to whom shall we go? Your words are words of eternal life. We have faith, and we know that you are the Holy one of God" (John, 6:68-69). St. Paul, in his first letter to Timothy, states: "For there is one God, and also one mediator between God and Man, Christ Jesus, himself man, who sacrificed himself to win freedom for all mankind, so providing, at the fitting time, proof of divine purpose" (2:6).

Jesus is also a number of times referred to as "Son of Man" who has also been given the right to pass judgment…" (John, 5:27-28). St. Peter's addressing Jesus as Holy means sacred, consecrated, devoted to God, but not divine; divine is reserved only for God! This, of course, is one interpretation of the true nature of Jesus: He comes from heaven and the "Son of Man," whose house is in heaven (3:14). It is interesting that in John's Gospel testimony, there is no mention of Jesus's earthly parents, Joseph, his father, and Mary, his mother, except for the Jews, when they argued against his messiah claim, saying, "Surely, this is Jesus, Son of Joseph; we know his Father and Mother" (6:42)—as a son of man, he definitely deserves no divine rank.

This, then, is Jesus as presented by the apostles, who knew him the best. But how do we reconcile this Jesus with the other Jesus, conceived by a Holy Spirit, born to the virgin Mary, in a manger to a father named Joseph; greeted by the three wise men; grew into a good and wise man himself, became a Rabbi, wanted to reform the Jewish faith; but was rejected, accused of inciting rebellion, tried, found guilty, nailed to the cross, died in pain and agony for the sins of men. Buried, rose the third day, revealed himself to his apostles, and after that went to heaven. This is why Christians everywhere celebrate his birth, Christmas Day, and his death, the crucifixion and resurrection, at Easter. Here, we have a unique and a special creation, with the participation of God's Holy Spirit; a man of purity, grace; goodness, truth, crucified, but resurrected, to show us that, yes, there is life after death, Fear not! The question is, which of the two Jesuses is the real one? Can they be reconciled, since the only thing that the two have in common is the "end"—their deaths. Their beginnings are totally at variance; one comes from heaven, is a mature "Man"; the other is born here on earth and grows up to maturity and his death on earth, as well. One worldly, the other heavenly; one sent directly by God; the other, perhaps, preordained to be, eventually, the messiah. One goes back to heaven—he calls it his home—after his crucifixion/resurrection; the other goes to heaven, for the first time, after his crucifixion/resurrection—a case of mortals crucifying a divinity; the finite overcomes the infinite!

This first Christian paradox, even though still resolvable, appears that the damage that it did/does is not as detrimental as one might expect; it is manageable by being celebrated only. But more importantly what is lost in the celebrations of a newly born special child is the conflicting emotions of guilt and redemption of Jesus's crucifixion and resurrection.

Be that as it may, let's turn our attention to the second Christian paradox that came close to, in effect, putting an end to the Christian faith at its very beginning. It happened as the Christians began to gain prominence due, primarily, to their tenacity and unshakeable belief in the correctness, the power and the promise of their faith—a faith based on and motivated by the love of their God for mankind; the sacrifice of his only son for their salvation; peace on earth and goodwill toward all men. This new force, based on peaceful resistance, coupled with Rome's inability to contain the Barbarian surge and push into and against the gates of Rome. This danger (in 313) forced the empire to recognize the right of the Christians to worship their God freely. The inevitable collapse of the Western Roman Empire forced Emperor Constantine to split the empire in two—the West and the East Roman Empires, with himself as the emperor of the Eastern part, the Byzantine Empire, which was to last over 1,100 years.

In 313 Constantine I gave the Christians freedom to worship their faith; and as an emperor, he believed in the ideal universal state; the unification of the earthy powers with the powers of the church/faith into one person—Constantine himself. He allied himself with the Christian Church/Faith, and as an emperor he was the head of the church itself. The alliance, in theory and expectations, looked sound and promising. However, it became evident—as time went on—that the characters of the two partners did not gel well; one earthy-raw power, disciplined to rule by force; the other, the power of divine faith, dealing with the salvation of souls, believes in peace and brotherly love. It was an alliance forged out of necessity and need.

Another event occurred within the church itself that proved even more catastrophic to the unity of the Christian Church than its uneasy alliance with a Roman emperor. The issue of Jesus's true nature came up again, but this time Father Arius questioned His divinity! This triggered a very divisive debate at a time of a faith in disunity and disarray—with no central authority but scattered dioceses with bishops in charge and their own "local" views of Christ Jesus. The disintegration of the church was imminent; something had to be done. The only person who could do something, and it was to his advantage to do something to restore unity, was the emperor himself.

In a big historical twist of fate, it was the old enemy—the emperor of the Roman Empire—who would now try to keep its old nemesis united and strong. Of course, he needed the Christians, their vitality, tenacity, and vibrant power, to help him save the Roman Empire—for he was still the Roman Caesar, with Roman ambitions, habits, and beliefs.

In 325, Constantine I summoned the first Ecumenical (Universal) Council at Nicaea to decide, not only the true nature of Christ Jesus but, in fact, the faith's most basic and fundamental tenets. The author of the *Story of Civilization*, Will Durant, in his Book III, Caesar and Christ, writes: Constantine became the sole emperor in 323, ruled for thirteen years, and at sixty-four years old, tired, the ruler died. "As his illness increased, he called for a priest to administer to him that sacrament of baptism, which he had purposely deferred to this moment, hoping to be cleansed by it from all the sins of his crowded life." This adjudicates that Constantine accepted and allied himself with the Christians for political reasons but was not one of them, and he "seldom conformed to Christian ceremonial requirements and cared little for its theology." A consummate politician and a brilliant general, he realized that holding an empire only by brute force is a shortsighted policy. He needed to soften the cutting edge of the Roman sword and thereby acquire the moral imperative to rule and rule as absolute monarch. The alliance with the Christians would give the "absolute" a human face, "for he was impressed by the comparative order and morality of Christian conduct; the bloodless beauty of Christian ritual; the obedience of Christians to their clergy, their humble acceptance of life's inequalities in the hope of happiness beyond the grave"(Durant). Perhaps, Constantine was hoping that some of these Christian attitudes and behavior would rub off on the Romans, help purify their morals, strengthen their social relations, and reduce the imbalance and hatred between the patricians and the plebeians—the class war! But more importantly for the Emperor, he realized that the Christians had no political power nor ambitions, for they were, so to speak, on another plane—the spirit plane; they were obedient and they followed the church and the ecumenical hierarchy and authority. This Constantine understood, and he saw mutual advantages to both church and state working together in unity in parallel lines.

Alliances of this kind, based on need and of necessity, may begin well, but as time goes by, they end up very badly, indeed; for their respective—in this case—opposing objectives prove to be irreconcilable and impossible to sustain. It is true that, thanks to the brilliant statesmanship of Constantine—and a few other emperor successors—the Byzantine Empire succeeded in extending the life of the Roman Empire by more than 1,100 years. At the end, the victory belongs to the meek, unambitious, peace-loving Christians. In time, most of Europe—including Russia—and the new world would become Christian lands.

In 330, Constantine "turned his back on Rome, consolidated his political and civil powers, began the building of his own capital, known to us by his own name—Constantinople. It was during this period that a "dark cloud" descended on his empire, but it was not from his own political branch of the government but from the Christians. In effect, three theological issues—known as: the monastic succession; the Donatist schism; and the Arian heresy—appeared out of nowhere and became very serious and in some instances dangerous. This crisis threatened the unity of the Christian Church, and, if allowed to spread and gather intensity, it would inevitably affect the stability of the empire itself—Constantine would have none of that!

He dealt with the threat swiftly and firmly; first, he dealt with the monastic succession that arose from the interrelations and interactions between the Christians and the rest of the world—their counterinfluence(s) on each other. "As the Christians sought converts, they mingled with people from all classes, including the rich, who lived well even on this earth; some Christians could not resist the worldly temptation, succumbed to it and became rich in their own right. The church itself was not too adverse to this, because it needed money to run the church itself. However, this propensity for worldly wealth went against the grain of the teachings of Christ himself; that God is a spirit, and the spirit above gives life, the flesh is of no avail, the baptized possess eternal life—they are the spirit-man. The influence of the relationship worked both ways; while the Christians converted the world, the world converted the Christianity, Christian monasticism arose, as a protest against this mutual adjustment of spirit and the flesh which leaned much towards the flesh" (Durant).

The minority who wished to stay true to the original Christian beliefs withdrew from the church and devoted themselves to purely spiritual pursuits—absorbed themselves in thought and contemplation of eternal life by renouncing wealth and pleasures of the flesh, since such tendencies are egocentric and evil. Some, like the Egyptian monk Anthony, sought refuge in isolated places; he lived by himself for twenty-five years, in full contemplation and devotion to Christ Jesus.

The Church was against such movement, not only because it was divisive but also because it was already moving away from the Buddhist influence of detachment as the means to salvation, and more toward the idea that Christ himself is the salvation of man. Later, however, it changed its position and saw monasticism as a countervailing force to greed for material possessions. Today, the existence of monasteries and the convents throughout the world is a shiny example of the survival and the endurance of the monastic movement, attesting to the lasting commitment of love and loyalty to Christ Jesus and His teachings!

The second issue that arose and threatened the unity of the church had to do with justice. Father Donatus—the bishop of Carthage—demanded that those who surrendered their beliefs during the period of persecutions of the Christians must be punished by losing their position of authority, and their previous church functions, e.g., baptisms, etc., should be rendered null and void. The church refused to impose such drastic measures. Donatus and his followers instituted a parallel, rival diocese, with their own bishops in the districts where the "cowards" were serving; violence and chaos spread, dividing the church. The evolving schism worried Constantine, since the instability of the church affected the stability of the empire.

He, in order to deal with the issue, called a council of bishops at Arles in 314, which confirmed its opposition to the Donatists, closed down their congregations, confiscated their properties and took away their civil rights. However, Constantine changed his position in 319, reversed the decree and restored all properties and civil rights, probably because of the 313 edict of Milan proclaiming religious tolerance to all faiths. The moral wisdom of the schismatics's' quest for justice was lost then, and it was repeated in the political arena in 1989; after the collapse of communism, the people of the free Eastern European countries wanted and expected that the former communists who participated in the torture, oppression and suppression of its innocent population must be held accountable for their crimes and punished accordingly—including being forbidden to hold future government position(s). The postcommunist governments failed miserably in their attempts—or lack thereof—to bring those opportunistic cowards to justice, as Constantine and his bishops did long time ago. As the innocent-pure in faith were made to suffer then, similarly, the innocent people of these countries are suffering now; for the former Communists, now Socialists, are in important governing positions and literally none of them were brought to justice.

Will Durant, the eminent and brilliant Historian, quotes Tertullian's short paragraph regarding the blood of martyrs, those that suffered and died, confirming the Christian belief: "There is no greater drama in human record than the sight of a few Christians, scorned or oppressed by a succession of emperors, bearing all trials with a fierce tenacity, multiplying quietly, building order while their enemies generated chaos, fighting the sword with the word, brutality with hope, and at last defeating the strongest state that history has known. Caesar and Christ had met in the arena, and Christ had won."

The third and probably the most important and significant theological issue Christianity has ever been confronted with is the nature of Christ himself. Man finds himself in a being of himself (full of limitations and constraints, except for his limitless imagination) that he does not understand nor like much. He spends much of his mature life trying to escape from himself and others like him; leans toward isolationism—escapes into the wilderness, gets detached from others; and becomes heartless, as he seeks to purge and overcome his evil passions. However, in the very process of acquiring absolute detachment, the intellectual and moral achievements have corollary moral results: for as you seek to expunge evil through detachment, you are at the same time casting out the other senses—pity and then love.

According to Arnold Toynbee in *A Study of History*, the philosophy of absolute detachment, carried to its ultimate end, defeats itself, because it denies man, himself. In denying the existence of the unity of man's natural duality of his being and consciousness, the sages's withdrawal from the real world of being spiritually goes nowhere and dissolves in the end in a negation of the nihilist philosophy of denial of all reality and truth. The soul, continues Toynbee, is left homeless and seeks to reenter the world of being—preserving it—unity in duality, as the nature of man requires. The homelessness of the soul caused by total detachment and renouncement of the being, with the sole intent to join and submerge itself in/with the totality of the supreme/universal spirit, leads to nirvana, not as Buddhism defines it as a state of eternal bliss, peace, beauty, etc., but a state of "a lifeless eternity of bliss"—a soul without a being. Christian theology totally rejects this view of heaven—man's final destination as being. It sees heaven as the place where the ultimate being resides with the living—loving—God.

The third issue that arose about 318 and escalated into a major crisis in the Christian Church was provoked by a priest from the Egyptian town of Baucalis when he shared his views about the nature of Christ with his bishop. The name of the priest, of course, is Arius, hence the issue became known as the Arian heresy!

Father Arius simply shared his views with his bishop by stating simply that Christ is not one with the Father; that is, he is not of the same substance with the Father/God. He argued that if the son had been begotten of the Father, it must have been in time; the son, therefore, could not be coeternal with the Father. Moreover, if Christ was created, it must have been from nothing, not from the Father's substance; Christ was not consubstantial with the Father. Bishop Alexander, shocked by Arius's views and their spread, attempted to resolve it by calling a council of Egyptian bishops; the attempt, however, failed. When Constantine heard of the situation and its potential consequences not only to the church but to the empire as well, tried himself a reconciliation between Arius and Alexander by writing a letter, in effect, warning both to reconsider their positions, but again, to no avail. Constantine, by 325, had enough. He convened the First Ecumenical—universal—Council of the church to resolve the question of what is the true nature of Christ. The council was held at Bithynian Nicaea, attended by more than 318 bishops and their retinue of lower clergy.

Will Durant explains what happened at the meeting: Constantine presided and opened the proceedings with brief appeal to the bishops to restore the unity of the church. There were two major protagonists with their respective posi-tions—Arius against the divinity of Christ, and Athanasius in favor of it. Arius reaffirmed his view that Christ was a created being, not equal to the Father but divine only by participation. Athanasius cleverly forced him to admit that, if Christ was a creature and had had a beginning, he could change; and that if he could change, he might pass from virtue to vice.

Furthermore, he made it clear that if Christ and the Holy Spirit were not of one substance with the Father, polytheism would triumph. However, he conceded the difficulty of picturing three distinct persons in one God; but he argued that reason must bow to the mystery of the trinity. At the end, all bishops, with the assent of the emperor, voted in favor of the trinity concept, with the exception of Arius himself and two of his supporters, who refused to sign the council's trinity doctrine.

The final version of the doctrine appears as a creed—The Nicaea Creed; it reads: We believe in one God, the Father Almighty, maker of all things visible and invisible; and in one Lord Jesus Christ, the son of God, begotten…not made, being of one essence (homoousion) with the Father…who for us men and our salvation came down and was made flesh, was made man, suffered, rose again the third day, ascended into heaven, and comes to judge the quick and the dead.

Arian and the two supporters were anathematized by the council and exiled by the emperor. An imperial edict ordered that all books by Arius should be burned and made the concealment of such books punishable with death.

Analysis of the Nicaean Creed shows that its theological doctrine, creating the concept of trinity in a world of faith based on and committed to monotheism—a belief in one and only one God—is unsound, unreasonable, contradictory and in conflict with Christ's essence as a savior of men and their Lord, rather than showing/presenting himself as a God, possessing and of the same substance as God is; and is one with God.

The creed begins, we believe in one God, the Father Almighty, maker of all things visible and invisible. This clearly states that Christian faith is monotheistic—one God, maker of all things; does not this include Jesus? And it continues, we believe in one Lord Jesus Christ, Son of God, begotten (procreated) not made, being of one essence/substance with the Father.

This statement is in contradiction of the first proposition—<u>one</u> God and creator of <u>all</u> things. God is one, he is pure, eternal, self-sufficient; creator of the universe, where Heaven exists. He does not, cannot and will not create a duplicate of Himself—since, such an action will denigrate the ultra-uniqueness of His oneness, and place His own authority at risk; Cronus made that mistake, begot Zeus and paid dearly for it. Christianity, certainly, does not want to slide down the path of recreating Greek mythology, for when we include the Holy Spirit in with God and God-Christ, we are indeed in the realm of polytheism. This is exactly what Athanasius was afraid of, that if we leave the three major characters as different beings, then that will constitute polytheism—hence, make all three of the same substances and having the same essence, and this will constitute Monotheism!

But, it is exactly here, at this point, where the council made its fatal error; since three different entities of/with different origins, degrees of hierarchical station and different in kind cannot all be divine—having the same substance. God is God, He is divine, absolute, and eternal; the Holy Spirit and Christ are not of His caliber and do not share his essence and, therefore, are not divinities in their own right—they are His loyal and obedient servants. Their relationship as different and separate beings is like our sun, its warm rays and their benefit to man.

The sun is God, the rays are the Holy Spirit, and Christ is the teacher who guides us how to best position ourselves to get the maximum benefit from the sun. The sun is not the same/one with the rays, the rays are not one with Christ, and Christ is not the sun—there is no polytheism!

The concern that the council had was that the unity of the church required that Christ himself—his nature—is of such caliber that he "exudes" and represents stable, firm, and constant character; for if the church admits that he is made—creature-like—like us the humans, he could change from good to evil. Here, a theological error is made; the holy/divine beings are designed to fit the needs of the church rather than adhere to the fundamental requirements of the Christian Faith; where is the stability and the constancy in that?

This concern is misplaced, since Christ Jesus already had established unquestionably impeccable legitimacy: God's emissary, coming down from God's kingdom and made king of God's living kingdom, God's gift to Him. What else could be more credible than that?

If we follow Jesus's sayings/sermons as represented by St. John the Baptist, the designated witness in the Gospel according to John, we can, to a degree, understand and be sympathetic with the council's deliberations. Jesus Christ, in his eagerness to save the human race, was too eager to define God as a spirit—the universal spirit (perhaps He should have paid attention to God's answer to Moses). But Christ claims more than that: He puts God in heaven, calls it God's kingdom—heaven, is therefore, a spirit kingdom; Christ places Himself in heaven, hence He is a spirit; claims to know God, calls Him his Father, and so on, and of course somewhere there is the Holy Spirit. Looking at all this, we have heaven—God's kingdom and His house; it is also Christ's house and of course the Holy Spirit has to be there.

But God is a spirit, hence heaven as a place/realm of existence suitable for spirit life, therefore, those that are in heaven and those that will go to heaven—for Christ promises that heaven is ours if we follow Him and His God—are themselves of spirit. From all of this spirit heaven, it is not too unreasonable to extrapolate and conclude that Christ is of the same substance—the substance being spirit—that He is a God. But this is a false conclusion because the same logic applies to all those—(assuming, at least that there is few)—in heaven are gods, which defeats the first basic tenet that there is <u>one</u> God; and that He is pure, eternal, indivisible, invisible, wise, wisdom, energy, and spirit. These are some of his characteristics and attributes, which do not define who or what God is; because once you define something, you are therein imposing on it limits and boundaries, which, of course, God does not have. To us, He simply is God that created the universe and everything that is in it, including men, where we exist for a purpose.

Viewing God as only a spirit residing in heaven whom the pure of heart will join, as spirit, resulting in a universe spirit, we enter the collective universality where each additional spirit adds to the total and forever pushing the total toward infinity—the meaningless universal total bliss—a bliss without individual beings to enjoy it. Heaven is a place of the highest realm of existence, full of the ultimate beings, for the ultimate purpose that God—above it—created and is its Lord.

Viewing Christ's faith in this way, perhaps Arius had it right all along that Christ is not of the same substance with God but is God's most trusted and loyal servant and as such God promoted him to an honorary/adoptive rank of Son of God—"Son of Man," which has nothing to do with essence (blood) relationship between the two, except in the minds of the council bishops, who needed to hold together a new, promising, and aspiring faith. The pressure of the imminent crisis and a Roman emperor who was familiar with the idea that emperors are divine, tipped the scales in favor of making Christ a divinity. The other motivating factor in favor of Christ's elevation is the very purpose of the creation and the existence of the Christian Church—the promise of eternal life in heaven and on Earth. "God's will will be done on Earth as it is in Heaven"

The will of God in entirely two different and incompatible realms of life is incompatible with the universal order of things. What is needed is an inter-mediary that is well established and influential in heaven with God, as well as on Earth and its people. Jesus Christ fits this requirement, since God sent him as an intermediary between man and God. The failure of his mission notwith-standing, the difficulty that arises and establishes another Christian paradox is how two natures—one human and the other divine—can in any real sense be present both at once in a single person.

The answer to this question has occupied Christian thinkers ever since the Nicaean Creed was approved. A number of theological proposals were pre-sented, but they did not really resolve the issue of Christ's duality. One such attempt believes that Christ's humanity was absorbed in his one divine nature; another maintains that even though he has dual natures, he operates with one will. Nestor, the patriarch of Constantinople, believed that Mary gave birth to a boy who grew up into a holy man and became Jesus Christ. In 553, the Constantinople Council, in an attempt to clarify the divine and the human natures of Christ, agreed that they are inseparably joined in one person and partake of one divine substance.

Arnold Toynbee, the author of *A Study of History*, believes that rather than concentrating on Christ and his dual natures, being God in spirit on the ulti-mate plane of existence, and being a Jesus Christ in flesh, taking care of God's business, we ought to find a common bond between God and man, an attribute

or a sense that man possesses, as well as God. And that thing/concept is love/
passion—it is "the most viable alternative that binds Man to his Creator; for
Man possesses love for his fellow men, is compassionate and generous, so does
God—because, if he does not, he is less than man, and that is irrational nonsense." So, the connection here is love, but how love here, love above, guarantee the connection between the two; when there is no visible physical viaduct
between the two; also, the absence of the propinquity principle being satisfied,
makes the love option highly inappropriate, for the task it must serve—Christ,
possessing dual natures, is most suitable since, as such, he meets both of the
above criteria. It is for this reason that the second coming of Christ is so vital
and greatly anticipated. In short, love is not a human attribute—emotion—that
God can rely on, since it is finite, unstable, and uncertain; it can easily turn into
hate. It is conditional, selfish, and egocentric; it is no match for God's love, pure,
eternal, constant, and altruistic—no comparison, indeed!

The most serious attempt in the reconciliation of science and the Christian
faith was made by Saint Thomas Aquinas (1225–1274) in his treatise On Being
and Essence, a metaphysical inquiry following Aristotle's logic—based on reason—who, like his teacher Plato, believed in the universe as an ideal world.

In the matter of being—the relationship between matter and form—St. Thomas
holds that they are distinct (only God is exempt from this rule); "separate,
neither matter nor form by itself is the essence of a physical thing. The form,
however, is the cause of the act of existing, for a thing comes into existence
according as it receives form. Still, the act of existing does not belong to form
alone; it belongs to the composite of form and matter. Together they constitute the complete principle by which a thing exists and is given its name of
being." Aristotle argues that form and matter are inseparable; and this union
becomes a principle by which he explained all growth, all movement. Motion
and change are the realization of form in matter.

It is true that that unity of mater and form creates a new thing; however, it does
not explain the very act necessary to begin the process of creation; there must
exist—as an a priori condition—the cause that acts upon the form to cause a
motion in order to achieve a change; for without the needed change being realized, the form and the matter will remain as they are.

In the totality of the universe, we are compelled to seek and find the vital first cause—the energy that starts the prime motion, causing change, flux; and it is in this universal flux that lies the source of not only creation but its differentiation. But all of these creations with differentiation is deliberate and for a purpose. It cannot be explained by mere chance that has no purpose. The purpose, of course, reflects a deliberate design, and behind the design stands a universal pure wisdom, coexistent with the universal pure energy that is the prime/first moving force—cause, constituting the universal vitality—the two are in one, hence, God/The Eternal Crown is of dual nature. As far as the being of man is concerned, it has nothing to do with the above. Man is a creation of nature; he is created as a whole being, complete in his own form. He is created in sufficient quantity and quality to fully develop his potentialities in order to exist in a meaningful and purposeful life. As a creature of God, once born, he cannot be altered by whatever external forces/means—for what God creates is Good.

As St. Thomas attests, regarding creatures, "If they exist, their act of existing is given to them by God…that is why in every creature, essence is really distinct from the act of existing, whereas in God the two are identical." God is purely and simply the act of existing; we need not fall into the mistake of those who assert that God is that universal existence whereby each thing formally exists. "The act of existing which is God, is such that no addition can be made to it. Consequently, in virtue of its very purity it is the act of existing distinct from every other act of existing."

This attempted synthesis between science and theology—for he believes that the Truth is indivisible—was accepted and became the official doctrine by Pope Leo XIII in 1879. However, succeeding pontiffs stayed away from it because, in effect, its logic counters the possibility of the existence of Trinity—since God is complete (the most complete), his purity, eternity, and self-sufficiency; he cannot be shared, altered, invaded, especially by others—lower beings—except as a reflection of His Being and/or as delegated to others by His essence! In fact, he maintains that everything is arranged in ascending order to God.

It is in the meaning and purpose of the creation of man that we must find the true meaning in the statement that God's will, will be done on Earth as it is in heaven! Man is created to do God's work on Earth and then, after developing his attributes and acquiring the required experiences, he will move on to the next, higher plane of existence until he reaches the ultimate (heaven) plane of being. Man, thus, begins the journey on Earth and completes it in heaven—the two ends of the same process—God's will is done on Earth as it is in heaven!

The next section deals in detail with man's journey to heaven—where he becomes the ultimate being!

Man's Universal Journey

We live in an interesting epoch of human endeavor: religion has weakened to the point of frustration, repeating the same old story that God will save us, but so far it hasn't happened and most probably it is not going to happen—ever! Science claims advancement; sends a new rocket into space, takes a few more pictures—in color—and with a few more experiments infers/extrapolates new findings, etc. All this notwithstanding, Darwin and the Big Bang ideas give us a small comfort, nothing of major significance. We find ourselves between the two opposing positions and are totally lost!

Science tells us that we come from matter via the evolutionary process and will die into nothingness. Lesson, live your life to the fullest, care not for anybody else, it is you that counts. Result, unbridled greed!

Religion just keeps promising salvation, but nothing has happened yet; and it isn't likely to happen. The cycle of birth, life, death moves on with the same results: suffering, struggle, fear, hopelessness, despair, agony, anguish, etc. There is too much pain in the world!

We seem to have forgotten that there is a purpose in human life. To discuss meaningfully the existence of the supernatural, creative power, we cannot rely only on faith, but we must make use of our scientific discoveries to give us the physical reality of the universal structure and operations; then, we can logically infer our beliefs—the intuitive transcendent awareness—and attempt to construct a universal system that brings together faith and science. Since both deal with the same reality, the only difference is in their approach. Science seeks the truth from the bottom up, whereas the revelationists claim to know the truth from the top down. Science seeks to discover what the believers already know! The two sides are convinced that their view is the correct one. The faithful believe that God exists and He created everything, but they fail to explain the origin of God Himself. Some argue that He created Himself; which makes no sense at all; why create the same God all over again?; there is no purpose in that. Science, on the other hand, relies on the Big Bang Theory to explain the origin of the universe, and evolution takes over to create the universe itself. This explanation is based on chance and all creation is without a purpose. Religion at least believes that there is a purpose for all the universal creation, even though they seem to be unsure what that purpose is, especially regarding man.

Science, nonetheless, confirms that, besides the existence of our own solar system, "there are more than 370 planets outside our solar system that have already been discovered…316 stars are confirmed to host one or more planets"—according to Dr. Timothy Ferris (*National Geographic*, December 2009).

This tells us that there is matter; and matter in motion gives energy; and since there are stars and planets that move according to universal laws and order, they in turn must reflect a universal design; universal design implies creation, and since creation without a purpose is a meaningless concept, then we can infer that all creation has a purpose—a particular/individual as well as a total purpose. If there is a universal purpose, then, behind it must exist a superpower that is its architect—the master architect of that creation and its purpose.

The creation of the universal existence consists not only of physical matter, but it includes the planes of Astral, mental, intuitional, the spiritual, and the nomadic—the ultimate being—and, of course, the creator and master of all things—the ultimate wisdom and energy. The top three planes are of such mystery to man that most likely we can never learn their true realities; we'll know of them as we go through the intuitional plane.

The creator of all things is in fact the eternal crown, consisting of two distinct but interconnected spheres—like the two sides of the same coin—one side is the pure indestructible energy; powerful beyond our wildest imagination, it is in fact the prime/first cause. The other sphere consists of pure and equally indestructible wisdom—the master designer and creator of the universe—indestructible intelligence is eternal, pure, invisible, the ultimate conscience, and with a single purpose—to design and create a perfect universe. A universe that is constantly evolving through the process of involution and evolution; the dynamic drama of unending change of universal differentiation.

In this universal totality, nothing really lives, nothing dies; there is only a fleeting moment of being. Thus, there is no beginning and there is no end, only unending change, as determined by the universal crown—the ultimate reality, which has no beginning and no end, eternal and indestructible. To the believer, a God; to the scientist, the first cause; but in fact it is both. A God because it is the creator of all, except itself; but not in the way religions expect it to be—a point of view of need; nor is it as science views the universe—purely a physical reality.

It is, in fact, the most perfect and purest being; possessing the supreme wisdom and the ultimate will, coentwined with the ultimate energy/spirit. It is also the ultimate universal conscience; this, however, is not the sum total of all the individual consciences—no such, collective conscience exists; conscience is individual only, and its purpose is to restrain or encourage man/beings on the other spheres from engaging in evil deeds or to motivate man to do good deeds to and toward his fellow men and his surroundings. Its unique nature places it as a separate eternal and all-powerful entity. It is on its own, self-sustaining; self-evaluating; self-re-directing and self-regenerating. The universe is its vision/project—of his choice—to design, to build, to mold into perfection—the realization of differentiation of wondrous, splendorous, things. It creates the major structures and foundations of the different planes/worlds of being; their interrelatedness and interactions. It also creates the conditions and the environments for the creation and the existence of beings and things. The needs and the cares requirements of the individual planes/worlds are left to their own will and wisdom. Each realm/world has its appropriate environment and inhabitants, clothed in appropriate bodies and possessing the appropriate state of consciousness.

The movement of the beings is upward, in an ascending order, from the lowest plane—the physical—to the highest plane—the nomadic, where the ultimate beings reside. The eternal crown is not accessible to beings! At the time of death, the self merely casts aside his or her garment and thereafter continues to live in the next higher plane—undergoes a metamorphosis—the Astral plane; the journey continues on till the self reaches the final—the ultimate plane—and proves that the self has successfully met and accomplished all the necessary requirements in all the previous planes; this is the final stop on our universal journey, the ultimate supreme being is realized. Its conscience is still individual, but it is universal in scope; its wisdom is second only to that of the eternal crown, and its transcendence is universal and real, unlike ours, which is "universal" but only intuitive.

The nomadic plane, as the final and supreme state of being, is in possession of, but not in control of, the lower three planes, i.e., the spiritual, the intuitional and the highest mental. It is the supreme self that embodies the will, the intuition, and the intellect. As we ascend into the next world, certain self(s) may be judged that their lower state of experience, knowledge, wisdom, and conscience is deficient, in which case it will be allowed to enter and stay on the next plane—in fact, no one is denied entry—but will be located in a lower station, where it will be given the opportunity to make up for the deficiency, and then—only then—it will be allowed to proceed to a full member of that world. In making up these deficiencies, and since they occurred on a lower plane of being, the deficient self (the evil), some believe, will be reincarnated back on earth in an animal form as punishment and then reborn as a human again. This sounds good from our justice point of view, but it is not possible from the point of view of the universe's structure and dynamics; the movement through the planes is upward to a better and more perfect plane; the opposite movement is contrary to that purpose and thus impossible to occur. And since the upper worlds possess the attributes of the lower (in different forms, of course)—and since the principle of interpenetration prevails among all planes, the needed deficiencies will be made up at the higher plane, the being's new residence. The penalty to the new self will, in time, be delayed/wasted and opportunities missed to gain access to a higher level of existence and much slower transition into the next better world.

It would seem that these propositions/views of the universe are in conflict with certain faiths and their beliefs; that there is hell, and there is heaven. The above views do not deny the existence of good and evil. They are there; it is how we deal with the evildoers that is different. It is the evildoer that will be judged to be deficient for full membership in the astral plane (the human in a spirit form) the sacrifice imposed on the deficient self in making up the deficiencies is its punishment, but this punishment is not an eternal one, as hell requires it to be! The Good Selfs will be rewarded by being placed on higher stations and their development is on a fast track. Nonetheless, the overall advancement of all selfs will be judged primarily by the performance of each self on the actual plane. Each plane of existence creates its own justice system and it has no influence or effect on the other planes. Its level of conscience will determine its degree of Justice.

The heaven is, in fact, our sixth plane, where and when the being reaches its ultimate being state, and in order to get there, we all must travel and go through the other five planes of being, step by step to the top. It must be made clear that this being journey through the realms/planes of the universe is not nor would it be an easy one; the fate of man is a unique and arduous one. It is man's destiny to fulfill this journey; since he is the one that possesses the very same attributes and capabilities that characterize the system of planes. He possesses the physical, the Astral, the mental, the intuition and the spirit, in, to be sure, significant amounts/degrees. He is capable, for he has the capacity to be molded/trained in acquiring the necessary experience and knowledge/wisdom to gain entry into the plane of the ultimate being.

The exact relationship between the crown and the ultimate plane is as it is between a master and a servant; the crown is the creator of all the planes/worlds and their interrelations and for each its own boundaries and independence, as per design. The ultimate plane, however, has no upward mobility; it cannot enter the crown's domain, since it is not pure, as the crown is, and is not eternal in the same sense as the crown is. They do not mix; the crown interpenetrates all, but none can penetrate the crown. The crown is not dependent on anything or anybody whatsoever; it is self-sustaining; it was there before it created the universe, so it is meaningless to suggest that it will become dependent on its own creation. It is not like the Father creates a son and in old age he becomes dependent on the son to take care of him. The crown does not get old—it is eternal—it is always what it is, and the universe being created is completely different. The crown has its own purpose/ends as well as its own means/assets, completely independent.

The principle of upward mobility, through the planes/worlds poses an interesting situation at the last plane—the ultimate plane—since mobility of beings stops there and all of us want to be there—the heaven—doesn't it get crowded there, and what is the outlet? If there is no outlet, then there is a danger that we may create a situation where the law of diminishing returns will set in, causing the average productivity to go down, turning heaven into hell! This concern, even though valid, is not likely to happen, since we have defined the crown as having infinite powers; it simply will expand the ultimate plane; since it is the closest to its objective of the perfect universe.

The crown is pure, perfect, and eternal; the universe is differentiated and divided into planes/worlds of specialized existences for the purposes of enabling the beings to acquire the necessary experiences, knowledge, and wisdoms to be able to eventually become the ultimate being—to live, as close as possible, in a perfect existence. This entails not only "living" in an "eternal bliss" but discharging its obligation to ensure that the upward journey of all beings through all the planes is carried out as per the crown's design. Viewing the universe in this way, we can meaningfully place and understand the significance of man's creation, as being in God's image. It is that God created man with the same attributes of the universe so that he may be able to move up to heaven. It is inaccurate to maintain that man looks like God. This is the humanization of God, which diminishes the greatness of God!

Man's universal journey constitutes an enormous endeavor, not only for man but also for God; and it is highly unlikely that he will undertake such a task for us alone; we can safely infer that there, in the outer reaches of the universe, "must" exist humanlike beings, most probably with much greater/superior attributes than our own. We are, therefore, not alone!

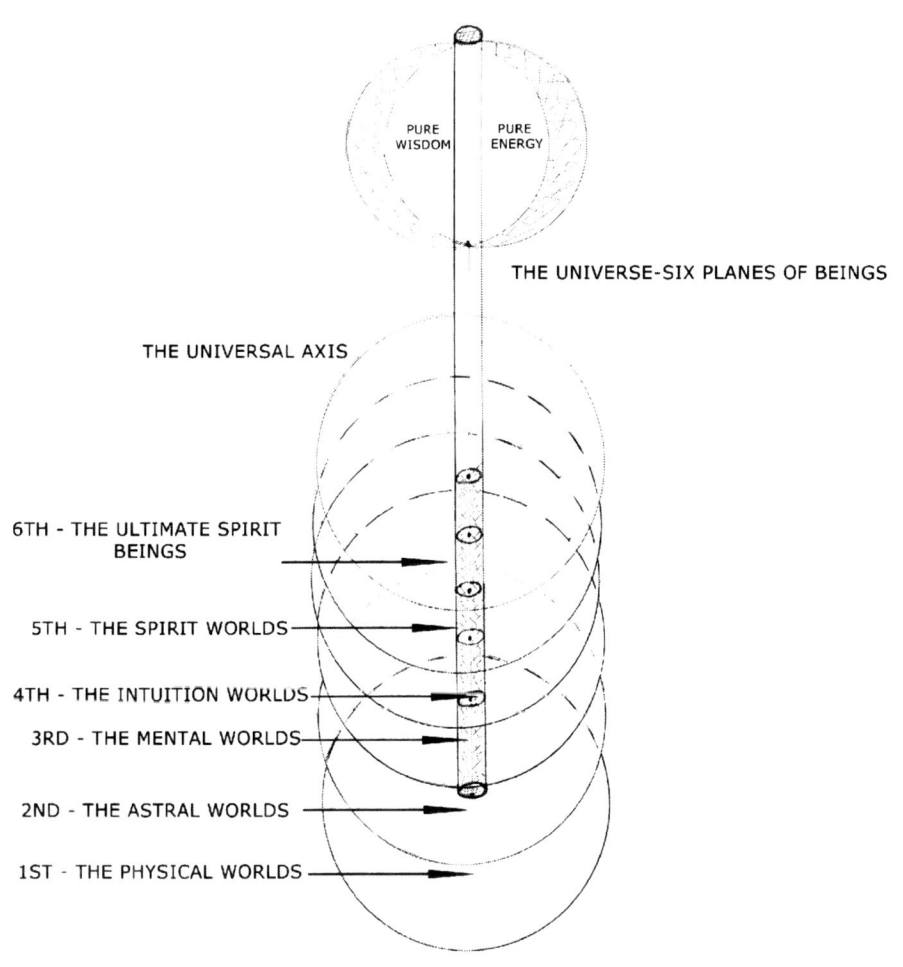

THE ETERNAL CROWN

PURE WISDOM   PURE ENERGY

THE UNIVERSE-SIX PLANES OF BEINGS

THE UNIVERSAL AXIS

6TH - THE ULTIMATE SPIRIT BEINGS

5TH - THE SPIRIT WORLDS

4TH - THE INTUITION WORLDS

3RD - THE MENTAL WORLDS

2ND - THE ASTRAL WORLDS

1ST - THE PHYSICAL WORLDS

PART II
THE ESSENCE OF CIVILIZATION

At the dawn of time, a caveman stood at the entrance of the cave. Looking out, he saw the light and felt the warmth of the sun; he saw the awesomeness of the land—its beauty and its vastness; he was moved to tears, he felt part of it, and said: this is my land, this is where I belong; I'll not perish, I'll live on it forever! Is this caveman's vision commitment and daring that reflects his will to survive, and with a conscience to carry out this commitment—his state of civilization?

Much later on, we see a man standing by the river Tigris, looking at the fields that he was plowing; he said—it is good—I'll stay here forever—this is my land!

After a long time passes, we see a man on the street of Hella's Athens—as he stood, looking about, he said, here I am, a human being, and went ahead and proved it; with determination, reason, imagination, intuition, will, and inner energy!

Now, we are in New York City, and we see a man standing on Fifth Avenue, looking at the window display, and he says: I want this now, and much more later; and there was more—he builds bigger and faster machines and bigger corporations to help him produce more—consume even more, on credit, and as he contemplates what to buy, he becomes aware that there are many more like him—today—than yesterday—he wonders about tomorrow!

These four men stood on this earth at different times and different places—representing vastly different epochs of human history—all four trying to survive and live, searching for meaning and purpose in their particular existence.

Who is the civilized one? Who shall say? And on what basis?

The first one saves the human race from extinction!

The second one gave man permanency, security—security from starvation, belonging, and being one with nature.

The third one gave us reason and the will to be free; to create beauty; to think, to inquire, contemplate, imagine not only our own reality of being but the universal reality as well.

The fourth one—the modern man—what does he do? He invents, innovates things—makes them bigger, faster, and makes them in mass, for mass consumption—use and throw away. He builds megacities, where we now live in the clouds—watching TV and "computing" on our PCs.

These four men, it seems, have very little in common; they represent different epochs of human history; where the means of survival are different; but their commonality lies in their nature of being the same species—the human kind—all dealing, struggling with the art of how to survive—live a life with integrity and purpose. The methods and the means are very different but the purpose is one!

The beginning of our civilization is very difficult to ascertain, precisely; however, it is connected with the time when man began to be aware of being different from the other living species and began to think and act as such—developing, with time, his own distinct and unique character. He realizes that he possesses different categories of being: the senses state of being; the mental state of being; and the psycho-spirit state of being. With this sense of awareness of his uniqueness, he, in time, established his complete state of differentiation; and with this "new" identity, he acquired "new"—innate—need to excel as a human being. He begins by concentrating on the development of his being—developing, acquiring an understanding of his environment and beyond—learning to apply this "new" knowledge/wisdom for the betterment of his own situation and that of his clan/tribe, etc.

It is somewhere during the time of his awakening and subsequent actions as a differentiated being that his civilizing process began—that is, when he could ignore the call of the wild. From this, we should not infer that this process of civilizing is either continuous or deterministic. It is a random thing—it begins, grows and falls—in different places/times in man's history. We cannot infer, just because we are the last ones, that our current civilization is better than all the preceding ones. There is no historical progressivity—for the differences in civilizations, chronologically speaking, is a matter of degree rather than of kind—since our potentialities and capacities as humans is one. After all, it was the Barbarians that put an end to the glory that was Rome!

The Dynamics of a Civilization

The explanation of how civilizations develop is based on the principle of duality of forces, which are contraries to each other, and yet are inseparable; neither can completely destroy the other. One force is passive, the other is active—the active acts upon the passive; and as a result of this clash, a change in the existing reality will occur, moving toward the creation of a "new" reality—that is, presumably, on a higher level of being/existence—hence, we have a progression—progressivity in the state of being. These "new" realities appear in different varieties: Empedocles—a Hellenic philosopher (490–435 BC)—believed that the universal changes are the results of such clashes—harmony vs. discord—"combine the indestructible material particles into varying forms—constituting the rhythm of the universe." The Chinese sinic world independently came up with a similar proposition/theory—the ying-yang process—the ying being the static/passive force; the yang being the dynamic/active force. Their interactions, however, is not that of the opposites; rather, each ascends into the other, reaches the point of no-further, and then the process reverses course, until the opposite point of no-further is reached. Thereafter, the flows become a series of permanent repetition. Example: light vs. dark—the shadows/darkness gives way to light, and light gives way to darkness. These type of opposites that ebb and flow off/to each other represent actual realities and their dynamics do not create new realities; its "constant" continuity is useful as a predictive tool—for example, the seasons and the like, situations that are determined by natural sources and forces, e.g., the sun, Earth's rotation, etc., that are a greater, planetary force—given realities, and as such, they in themselves have no self, no voluntary actions or reactions, to each other. Their pattern of behavior is already determined—establishing their precise, repetitive pattern/rhythm of behavior. Since these "dualistic" forces are a function of other, greater forces and have no deterministic action of their own, it is, therefore, pointless to categorize them as dualistic contraries.

If, on the other hand, we take the universe—representing the origin and the prime source and energy—then the contraries principle will apply; since the interaction/clash between the opposites; static vs. dynamic; integration vs. differentiation; definite vs. indefinite; finite vs. infinite, etc., (as H. Spencer points out) will result in an identifiable and predictable pattern/ rhythm of creation and destruction of the new and the old worlds/planes!

There is, however, another school of thought that attempts to explain reality by the process of dialectics; whereby the clash of the opposites will create a motion, and that motion, in-turn, will cause a change in the now reality—whatever that change is, it represents our new reality. Empedocles began this line of inquiry, but he did not develop a convincing method to support his argument—as I stated before, he said that two opposing forces combine indestructible material particles into varying forms—i.e., creation of new reality. Friedrich Hegel (1770-1831), the German philosopher, developed what we know today as "The Hegelian Dialectic," which had an enormous world influence, especially to the Socialists. Marx, using Hegel's dialectical reasoning as a basis, developed his own dialectical materialism theory. Hegel maintains that there is a universal perpetual self-creating process driven by the envelopment of the absolute. The perpetual rhythm of creation, on ever-rising levels, indicates a qualitative progressivity, but this improvement is at the expense of the previous "lower" level of existence. This is the universal dynamics—where for the new to exist, the old must die. This principle precludes the possibility of a universal differentiation, and universal expansion; the two fundamental characteristics of universal reality—for there is no universal beauty without their existence!

The logical process of his dialectics consists of the opposites: there is one concept, the thesis, and there is also the antithesis, whereby they inevitably will interact and create the synthesis—the new reality, the new thesis, which is on a higher level of being/existence; and it has its own opposite—the new antithesis, where they in turn will collide and create new opposites—this renewal process of creation and destruction repeats itself indefinitely, continuously, creating new reality(ies), but at the expense of the existing reality—the thesis, which is "no longer a being," that is, "the idea of being evokes the idea of not being"—the old dies so that the new may exist. It is the current/now thesis that is the absolute and is the active partner in the process—it envelopes the passive partner, the antithesis, into submission, resulting in a new thesis—reality. It is very much like when the soul envelopes/yokes the body, creating the spirit-man, moving "from aesthetic contemplation to that of a moral responsibility"—an act of faith— "the realization of man's spiritual progress." Hegel sees this spiritual development in a historical perspective, and as a "necessary manifestation due to the clashes of cultures," whereas Kierkegaard sees it as a "free will" in action, "where every man must decide for himself whether he will do the ascendency"—it is by "direct intuition" that one can "understand his own self." That is, only by "immediate experience"—passing through "dark night of the soul"—in anguish, can we know what it means "to be or not to be"—knowing your own conscious existence. Not, as Hegel wants us to believe, that it is a continuous clash of the opposites going through a mechanized process of dialectics.

These two approaches attempt to explain the nature of human experience: one sees man as a free, thinking and acting being—charting the course of his life, according to his desires, beliefs, and means, and as a result of these efforts, he will discover, know, and understand his own being—and thereby develop his capacities and potentialities, realizing his own self, residing in a common environment, pursuing a common purpose—the creation of a more perfect civilization—advancing the human condition!

The other approach explains human development in deterministic patterns of behavior between opposing forces, clashing in predetermined phases, resulting in and creating new realities. The individual, here, is lost; he is simply an actor in a play—he is not real—he is simply reacting to an already, predetermined (scripted) reality, a reality that is not of his own making. Where is his human interaction and interrelation with other human beings as human beings? It does not exist, because he is not a free man; in fact, he is chained to the dialectic method, which is the true reality!

Karl Marx—the most extreme social theorist (1818)—adopted Hegel's dialectic method, but he departed from Hegel's cultural clashes and established his own theory of dialectical materialism, which explains the nature of social change.

It argues "that matter is the true reality, and everything else is derived from matter—and is thereby, explained in terms of matter." Life, he claims, is a "series of contradictions—a negation of negation, present in both things and processes." Marx's main/central idea is that motion, due to the clash of the opposites—thesis vs. antithesis—causes motion, and that, in turn, causes change; the resultant—the synthesis—is the new reality (but at the cost of the current thesis/reality).

This universal and social dynamics of a continuous transformation of reality fails, at least in three respects: First, it fails to explain the beginning of the first thesis. Second, how did the antithesis become a reality?; and how did the process—the clash of the two—begin?; there must have been a first cause to begin the unceasing process of transformation—the universal dynamics! Neither Hegel nor Marx provides us with a reasonable explanation. Then, how and on what basis do we justify the transference of a scientific determinism of a physical reality to apply/ transfer to a social setting constituted of human beings. If there is anything that defines man, it is that his behavior is uncertain and, therefore, unpredictable. Dostoevsky underlines the truth of this position by stating that the most difficult task man is faced with is to make choices, by creating options and choosing the best; but is the best the right choice?—the selection process carries its own collateral consequence(s)—this is man's irresolvable dilemma! Dialectic reasoning promises to free man from these dreaded decisions—correct man's human weakness by applying the dialectic method. Marx, in fact, is exploiting this human weakness in order to gain the political loyalty and support from the working class—the proletariat—setting class against class—the proletariat, pure, hardworking people, exploited by the vicious-evil-greedy capitalists—whose dialectic time, as the thesis, has run its course; it is time for a new socialists' thesis, followed—in time—by the ultimate social thesis—communism. That is, a state of existence where each citizen would have reached a level of consciousness—in the ethical sense—that he will take only what he needs and work according to his ability. It is then, and only then, that the "Laws of Social Activity, realized by the proletariat class, will triumph over the, hereto, dominant Laws of Nature"— Marx's proletariat triumphs over his dialectics—an irony, indeed!

It is, indeed, a mystery of the irony to claim that the fallible triumphs over the infallible, where the natural law determines progressivity; whereby, just because of the efforts of the proletariat (the least pretentious) class, is capable of reaching a perfect social state; that can overrule his scientific theory of dialectic materialism. This is a theory that sees no end to its dynamic process—a process of "continuous" progressivity, operating in an infinite "span" of time, otherwise, it becomes invalid by its own logic of negation—perfection is not a state of being, it is a state of always becoming better!

The collapse of the Soviet Union and China's orientation toward "guided" capitalism prove that Marx's dialectic materialism and its corollary—the idea of communism—is the greatest historical fiction ever written by a man. Arnold Toynbee—the English historian—himself holds a similar duality point of view, but he calls it the "Challenge and Response, sequence of events, that cannot be predicted with certainty." However, he adds a divine element into the essence of civilization, stating: "I do not believe that civilizations have to die…civilization is not an organism. It is a product of wills". Moreover, "it has a purpose, a duly perceived but divinely ordained purpose." Dr. Toynbee concludes, "History is a vision of God's creation on the move." This creation—drama that takes place in the universe—is the result of the interaction between the static and the dynamic forces; it is continuous clashes that establish an identifiable pattern of continuous behavior—the rhythm of creation and destruction. Dr. Toynbee believes that similar rhythmic patterns exist and prevail in our quest to become civilized human beings. That is, civilization and its progressivity, like the universal progressivity, is a function of the process of the inherent conflict that exists between the contraries—the clash between "static condition and the dynamic activities,"—is and constitutes the fundamental condition that the development of a civilization(s) rests upon. This sense of dualities at work is best illustrated and represented by the sinic "ying-yang" symbol, as the most apt, according to Dr. Toynbee, who states: "because they convey the measure of the rhythm direct and not through some metaphor derived from psychology or mechanics or mathematics."

Dr. Toynbee's process of civilizing—the "challenge-response" relationship—sounds more applicable to human interactions, but it is misleading, since changing a name does not change the nature of the process itself, especially if we take into account that the creation and the development of a civilization is "divinely ordained and its purpose is duly perceived." This, even though it represents a theological determinism, shows that his challenge-response process is much more deterministic than he cares to admit.

Besides, there is his assertion above that "history is a vision of God's creation on the move." Regarding the sequence of events due to the challenge-response mechanism, it is important to point out that the acting forces are human beings—it is a clash of human-dynamic force acting upon another human-static force, leading to an outcome of winners and losers—the victorious are the creators of civilizations, and the losers are swept into historical oblivion. This view of the civilizing process makes it a function of the existence of a crisis environment—e.g., class struggles. Such proposition is grossly inaccurate, since the civilizing process is based on human creativeness—a function of man's systematic application of his most inner forces and his will power to excel!

> Beauty, in thought, idea and image, cannot be destroyed;
> You, can kill the Artists but, you cannot kill his Art!

Civilizations, I believe, are the consequences and a product of human effort; they are not ordained nor controlled by the supernatural—nor do they have divine purpose—divine purpose does not change nor fall, civilizations do change and fail. God, really, does not enter nor interfere with our human intercourses and interactions—that is why he gave us free will—to act but with consequences.

Civilization entails a collective human effort in creating a framework of social structures whereby people will live by the rule of law, in freedom of thought and action, reflecting the reality now and the aspirations that it strives to achieve tomorrow—that is, it defines man in a social setting in two ways—you as being, and tomorrow as becoming. The subject is man, the object is his becoming; the two are separate by time but are inseparable by essence, since man as a being cannot be defined as a moment in time; but is defined as a connected series of moments in its totality. The human life is predetermined and it has an end—that is its nature. The life of a civilization is uncertain; it is not preordained; therefore, it has no nature of its own. It is a product of man's taught, effort and will—it is what man makes it to be; that is its essence. It serves man's purpose; it is man's means toward his purpose. It is that—that, is, moving through time, the relationship between the subject and the object, creating outcomes, good or evil—that defines man as a human phenomenon of being!

Civilization can be viewed as having identical patterns in its evolving—the "creative" process of becoming, and eventually of being, if the objectives are realized—however, it has no definitive end as man has. The difficulty with history is that we see and study man—his civilization—in antecedent order, rather than in its natural order of development; and since we know—already—its final outcome, we miss a great deal of its evolving journey of becoming. It is in the evolving process of becoming that the civilization's creations/destructive urges reside. The evolving process of creativity is the conflict between what is—customs, tradition, habits—and what is missing/desired. The urges to redress the missing/wrongs of society challenge the status quo, creating a conflict—struggle ensues—the series of such conflicts will determine the state of civilization—the transition between yesterday, the past, and tomorrow—the future is the responsibility of today—now; yesterday is history, tomorrow is uncertain, today is real, but the time is so short!

Dr. Toynbee maintains that human "history is not a sum total of series of forces at work, but a series of human relationships, which create a change, and in this change, it is hoped, will be a creative one, that will shake part of mankind out of the "integration of custom" into the differentiation of civilization."

All things change, but not at the same constant rate, and, therefore, in time, imbalances will occur, in our goals, in our means and in our motives, that will inevitably alter the fundamental foundation on which the hopes and the expectations of the new generation(s) rest. New generations are born, grow and mature, bringing with them: new ideas; new thinking; new desires; new needs, new hopes; new inventions and new ambitions, etc. They will formulate their own visions of their tomorrow, with their own commitment of energy, will, and conscience to carry out this commitment.

All civilizations are different and unique in their own right; but they all share three things that are common to all: their beginnings start with an "idea—a purpose"; their beginning and becoming processes are similar, if not identical, and they all face their inevitable end, and only the duration of time varies. Civilizations are unlike the confluence of tributaries of small rivers joining together to form the great river; they, individually, have created something unique that succeeding civilizations have benefitted from—but only as means and not as foundations that constitute an a priori condition(s) for the development of the new civilization(s). Historical continuity of all civilizations is an illusion, based on the idea of class conflict—propagated by the communists.

Nonetheless, we gain enormously by their ideas, discoveries, and experiences, which we incorporate in our lives. From the Chinese, we learned the concept of money—which moves our commercial world; their discovery of gunpowder that the West turned into a military weapon. From the Hebrews, Moses gave us the Ten Commandments—which is the basis for our sense of morality, and the idea that there is only one God. From the Arabs, we learned the importance of the zero; the idea of immortality—that is the foundation of all faiths; their use of hieroglyphic writing led to the development of our Western alphabets—which enabled us to develop our unique and distinct language, which defines and expresses our national history and future aspirations. Hellenes taught us the idea of beauty, individualism, democracy, the sense of universal ideas, laws that are immutable, etc. Romans taught us that one man cannot rule the world based on the idea that might is right, and that the unity of any state/empire cannot be maintained if that state/empire is divided into two classes—patricians and the plebeians. The early Christians taught us that faith in God is the greatest force of all!

The above are a few but important examples of what we have inherited from past civilizations—they constitute the common threads that bind us all as human beings—they are the means/lessons that we adopted or failed to adopt to help us develop a better world. In our journey of discovering the truth, we have gone through different ages and phases of human interactions to achieve that goal. The struggle has been between those that rule and the masses that they rule—oppression against freedom!

The Purpose

The real purpose of a civilized society is the realization of the following objectives for its people:

<u>One</u>: Fulfillment—the required condition for the uplifting of the human spirit, enabling the individual to live a meaningful life and in time discover life's purpose.

<u>Two</u>: Enlightenment—the necessary condition for the realization of man's Essence.

<u>Three</u>: Refinement—the required condition for the enablement of man's soul.

<u>Four</u>: Faith—man's eternal hope—for eternity—that sustains his purpose in life!

<u>Five</u>: The Nature of man—his:
- A. Life—the state of Being
- B. Liberty—the condition of Being
- C. Essence—the purpose of Being

These are, then, the necessary factors for man to acquire in order to fully develop and achieve complete understanding of one's own condition as a civilized human being.

Motives

Generally speaking, it is accepted that man is motivated by two distinct and separate motives. The first is our sense of morality. It is faith-based, our belief in divine authority. Our nature is divinely inspired and determined, and, in that sense, we have a speck of the divine in us—call it will or conscience or both. Whatever it is, it is the force that enables us to know and understand what is "good" and what is "evil." They are the opposites of each other and are not the absence from each other. As opposites, they are in conflict—war—with each other; and since both are part of our being, they, in turn, determine our behavior. If our acts and deeds are of the good kind, we are said to be good, and if our acts and deeds are of the evil kind, we are said to be evil. Goodness reflects God's goodness and kindness, and, if we emulate them, we'll be blessed with His grace and go to heaven. Evilness, on the other hand, reflects the devil's evilness and depravities; and if we act accordingly, we'll end up in hell forever. Whether we go to heaven or go to hell depends—solely—on the individual; he or she decides how to act and behave; these decisions are not easy; they involve our innermost emotional, agonizing, conflicting, and contradictory feelings, which make it impossible to know, with certainty, what is good and what is evil. This struggle reflects and constitutes the essence of our morality—the strongest and the most enduring motive of human behavior—that is of global proportions and historical endurance. Its strength and endurance lie in the fact that it straddles and connects the finite with the infinite and our material world with the world of tomorrow—the spirit world!

The second motivating force is man's ethics, arising from his inner instincts and drives—the need to survive—instinct that causes man to be egocentric. And it causes, on-the-other hand, his propensity to procreate—the force that causes man to be altruistic—a life/existence with others, in a common social setting, under collective social rules—your actions must be in consideration of others. It is in this collective environment where the individual is cautiously placed in conflict with his own inner feelings and drives; and in order to resolve this conflict between his need to survive egocentrism and his desire to exist with others—altruism—he is forced to seek a balance between the two, but that balance is possible only if the individual—willingly or by compulsion—is ready to compromise, but comprise is, indeed, difficult. Egocentrism is a very powerful motive for/of behavior, since it is based on and reflects a very basic and simple reality—the truth is that if I do not look after myself—my interests—nobody else will—for the I to survive and live well, the I must look after itself. This fact splits the I from the collective whole—it is a case of I vs. them! And in order to survive in this world, I must acquire power, influence and prestige by amassing wealth—by being greedy. But greed is the very antithesis to altruism—the fundamental condition for the creation and the existence of any society. Therefore, for any society to survive and flourish, it must apply coercive methods to reduce and possibly eradicate the greed-based motives that split the harmony of the collective whole—but the method(s) used "may" punish and penalize the creative excellence of the motivated few! The "collective will" has yet to find a convincing, simple argument to serve as a motivating force—for all of its members—to induce each member to apply himself as if he is working for his own interest; unfortunately, as of now, such incentive does not exist.

Attempts have been made to appeal to our sense and belief in humanity—we are all brothers—hence, we are all our brothers' keepers—a sense of generosity and obligation—this becomes awkward to both the giver and the receiver—the giver feels good and superior and the receiver feels inferior and loss of dignity. The appeal based on morality—be kind to our fellow man—is a faith-related concept and is based on selfish motives, to enhance your chances of getting into heaven. These are motives that evoke pity rather than purposeful and noble action(s).

Altruism, as a civilizing motive/force, leads one to conclude that the welfare of the individual is a function of the will of all, and the moving force—the social dynamics—is adaptation. The opposite applies to egocentrism; as a motive/force to civilize, it leads one to conclude that the survival of all is a function of the creative excellence of the few; and the driving forces here are the quest for gain and competition. Creation and the development of civilizations are possible, but only when the positive/creative forces/drives of morality and ethics overwhelm and prevail over their negative/destructive counterparts: that is, when goodness penetrates and mellows the inner drives of the individual, thereby directing his creative impulses toward constructive acts and deeds. To supplement the civilizing drive, the process must be complemented by an equal creative drive and direction by the state to offset the evils' detrimental penetration into the ethics of social conduct. Society, therefore, must find and implement countervailing measures to dampen—eradicate, if possible—such destructive influences acting on the social fabric. These corrective measures, however, must not be done at the expense and the detriment of the positive/creative motives and influence.

The balance between egocentrism and altruism—i.e., fairness and motivation—must exist, but it ought never be tilted against the individual, for it is his will and conscience that constitutes civilization's drive and energy.

Sources

In order to achieve the stated objectives that civilization demands, motives alone are not enough. We need resources—natural, human, social and spiritual—that will enable us to provide the necessary goods and services for the satisfaction of the stated objectives. The natural resources—land, water, climate, raw materials, gas, oil, machinery, transportation markets—constitute our opportunities, but their shortages will determine our limitations as well. Their efficient application in the production of needed Food is of vital importance, since it will determine the extent to which society will be able to free its labor force to pursue more creative endeavors in an urban setting or environment, rather than remain on the land to produce just enough to feed oneself. The development and the existence of an urban life is a function of the rural efficiency to produce sufficient surpluses to feed the urban population and thereby enable it to remain urban.

The efficient use—the allocation and the coordination—of all of the resources will be done by human effort, which itself will have to be trained to deal with a variety of skills that will be required to enable the state not just to produce and distribute the finished goods and services, but also to allocate efficiently its labor force in a way that will ensure the development of a civilization that it has envisioned for itself. In the pursuance of this goal, the society must establish the required social framework of institutions, creating the positive environment to ensure that the individual is free to follow his own independent course of action—in determining his life, his faith, his thoughts, hopes, and dreams—in a free and open society that values human life, dignity, and respect!

Built-In Constraints

We can also define civilization as man's journey through time—living in a collective environment where he, as an individual, is continuously challenged to readjust his attitude, belief, and actions to an ever-increasing collective whole; as the collective whole gets bigger and bigger, he, in respect to it, gets smaller and smaller, where his stature and significance diminishes accordingly, thereby creating a society comprised of weaklings. As a consequence of this, a degradation in the creative pool will occur, reducing society's creative will and energy, which is the essential ingredient required for a steady development of a civilization. Here, we find ourselves in a paradoxical dilemma—as the collective whole increases, its creative pool of energy and willpower decreases;

the two forces are inversely related, since their needs to "exist" are opposite to each other. For the collective whole to function effectively, it requires and rests on discipline, uniformity, and order; whereas, the creative genius requires and rests on freedom and individuality. One requires stable centripetal motion to hold the whole together; the other thrives on centrifugal motion to shake up the status quo—to move society in a more dynamic state of social action and individual interactions in order to establish a new, more progressive direction. To avoid sliding into this built-in social dilemma, it is necessary that a harmonious balance between the two forces is established and maintained, to ensure the progressive development of its own civilization.

The other built-in civilizing constraint—related to the above but is more Kafkasian in nature—deals with the system's centralization of public and industrial services and its effects on the individual—his attitudes, behavior, and performance. The process of human interaction is subjected to overburdening man, with mass institutionalization of human life—which lends itself to the cause-effect analysis; whereas human interactions are based on the challenge and response series of actions. These two realities exist in the same collective environment, dominated by the powers of centralizations, where even though they are staffed with human beings—who act as tools for the incorporated entities—they become more inanimate, impersonal—unfeeling/soulless instruments of the public and the industrial will. The individual, in this mass world, becomes isolated, insecure, anxious, and hopeless. All this causes him to become more and more self-absorbed—egocentric—satisfying his instinctive needs at the expense of all the other requisites for a meaningful human existence.

The next impediment to a steady growth of a civilization is the generation gap—the now generation always rejects the ideals, values, beliefs, and achievements of the previous generation as being outdated, out-of-style, passé, and more or less irrelevant. They are fascinated by the "new"—it is accepted as better; and yet they do not know the long-term consequences of everything new that is a result of science and technology—e.g., the invention of the car, at the time, was seen as a deliverance—freeing man from the horse-moving man, one more level away from the animal world—and it was an example, a marvel, of man's progress; but now it is viewed as a dangerous pollutant and a necessity to earn one's living. The creation of things in mass and the building of things on a mega scale is unsustainable, contrary to human nature, and insanely waste-ful—the new is infinite, but our resources are finite! Instead of doing all we can to curb man's appetite for more—his egocentrism—to prevent the impending disaster, we are, on the contrary, doing everything possible to encourage him and keep him doing the wrong things—even financing his mass consumption indefinitely, burying him in debt.

The disconnect between the past, the known, and the future, the unknown, is an interesting phenomenon. The known can be criticized, praised, but it cannot be changed—the sacrifice/cost has already been made—it is what it is! The future, on the other hand, is unknown; it can be what you wish it to be—idealized, hopeful, and, perhaps feared. It is a built-in confidence and exuberance of youth to prove itself that it is stronger, brighter and better than the older generation— it will succeed where the old failed; it will build a better world for all. This urge to excel is based on some sort of ego-trip—"I am better than you," or perhaps it reflects an accumulation of suppressed inner feelings and frustrations of failures and insignificance—as exemplified by father-son-mother-daughter relation-ships. This conflict takes place now, but the relationship between the combatants is a generational one—it is between the past, tradition, and the future, change. That is, what is vs. what is to be; the certain vs. the uncertain. The promise of tomorrow, of course, has its own dramatic appeal—everything is possible; how-ever, youth forgets that the foundation of the uncertain tomorrow is the certain yesterday—tomorrow is impossible without yesterday, hence, yesterday is an a priori condition for the existence of tomorrow, and, therefore, it cannot be rejected as irrelevant—few sons have rejected their father's inheritance!

The new generation infers that everything they do and create is better than what the old generation did—that there exists a direct relationship between what is new and what is better—i.e., the new qualitatively is superior to the old. That is, that there exists a progressivity in the human condition. This pro-gressivity argument, based on science and technological advancement, makes "some" sense, in terms of a higher standard of living (for a limited few) reflect-ing material consumption, but it does not, in any meaningful way, imply that we as human beings—in terms of our quest for a meaningful existence and purpose in that existence—are better off today than our forefathers yesterday. Just because we live longer and there are many more of us does not mean that we are better human beings—I would suggest that the opposite is the case.

Whatever the case may be, the conflict is unnecessary and disrupts the steady—uninterrupted—development of our civilization.

Another impediment that adversely affects the development of a civilization is based on and reflects our sense of spirituality—that aspect of our inner motives/drives that propels us to reach out and touch the stars; to escape the confines of our earthy limits. Our faiths/religions give us the opportunity to do just that—reach the heavens—but it extracts a heavy price. It gives you a promise, but there is always a condition—which works on our conscience, that we are evil because we are animalistic, the flesh-man, that unbearable egocentric characterization—which we cannot escape nor accept. Man is born naked and alone—nature, made him so—he is himself and for himself, for his own survival. He is against the rest of the world—he can never win, a fact that makes him always insecure and suspicious of others and their motives. His nakedness reminds him of his animalness, and that fact makes him ashamed of himself, hence the need to cover his nakedness; thereby, the realization of a greater differentiation from the rest of the other animals.

Cover all you will, the body is the same—it does not change. The perception of a naked body as being shameful is shared by the Jerusalem-based faiths, for different reasons. The Christian Church holds that man at birth is incomplete and deficient—he is a flesh-man, and as such he sins; he has no spirit, therefore, he possesses no will nor conscience. He is more animalistic than human—he is a savage/barbarian, and as such he is incapable of being civilized!

To become civilizable, he must become a whole—i.e., the spirit-man. He must go through a process of initiation and purification—through immersion in or sprinkle with water, the Christian rite of baptism. This rite, in fact, entails the rejection of evil, the devil, and the acceptance of the good, Christ, the Lord and the Savior. The initiated, after being purified with the holy water and blessed with the Holy Spirit (and most likely given a new name), is now the spirit-man; and with this baptism, he receives two gifts from God—free will and a conscience. With all this, he is now a complete and sufficient man—i.e., he is a completely differentiated human being. The transformation from the flesh-man to the spirit-man entails the Christian belief that there exists homeless souls that seek homes of their own. The Holy Spirit blessing—as the key component of the baptism—achieves exactly that; it unites the homeless soul with the now "new" man—i.e., the spirit-man. The two entities are now completely compatible to cohabit, to exist in one body, as one. This is achieved presumably by the process of "dialectics," whereby the homeless soul, acting as an antithesis to the flesh-man, the thesis, by enveloping him, causes a new creation, the synthesis, which is the "new" spirit-man. This process, however, may not be entirely true, since it goes against the doctrine of God's creation. God "creates the world. This world is not God; but it is not evil because it is not God. Being God's creation, it is good" (R. Niebuhr).

The two gifts that Christians receive with their baptism are a very significant aspect of Christian doctrine. The gift of free will enables the Christian now to take control of his own destiny—the self-determination principle. This principle, however, is based on strict obedience of the Christian doctrine—its tenets/creed; failure to comply with this requirement carries grave consequences—denial of entry to heaven—with redemption possible in extreme circumstance(s). This gift of free will—self-determination—shifts the onus and the responsibility to the individual for his thoughts and actions—if he chooses wrongly, he will pay for it, if he chooses right, he will be rewarded accordingly—a principle of behavior based on reward and/or punishment. The flesh-man was not confronted with such a dilemma of choice; he, as incomplete and insufficient, could not be expected to make the right choice, due to his deficiency in his own creation—it is God's fault that he could not differentiate between what is good and what is evil and act accordingly.

In fact, the gift of free will gives you the right of choice, but this in itself does not guarantee the right choice. The right choice is based on the second gift—the possession of a conscience—which will save him from sinning; since now he is a spirit-man, he is part of the Holy Spirit and as such he knows the truth—an a priori condition necessary for making the right choice—he chooses good over evil!

Thus, the Christian theological doctrine resolves the problem of egocentrism. But does it? It, in fact, may have been encouraged by the free will gift—giving the individual the right of self-determination—reinforcing the instinct of survival, which is the prime cause of egotism and splitting the I from the rest of the world, disturbing the universal unity and harmony—the relativity principle. The conscience gift may not be sufficient to offset such strong tendency, since it is based on the a priori basis of knowing the truth to make the right choice. However, knowledge of the truth implies and infers knowledge of God and His will. Sadly, such knowledge on an individual basis does not exist! At best, we have an abstract "notion" of the existence of such a reality. Moreover, it is very doubtful that man—physical vs. spiritual—has any universal reach to adversely affect its harmony and unity—this influence belongs to God and God alone.

There is no doubt that a selfish—egotistic—man stands in the way of collective unity and harmony, conditions required for the development of a stable and progressive civilization. To what extent the emergence of the cross succeeded in dampening egocentrism's adverse effect(s) is, of course, debatable; but we cannot simply brush aside its failures/excesses—even today, the greatest demonstration of greed for material wealth resides in countries of the Christian faith. Also, science—which questions/disclaims God's existence—is prevalent in the same Christian lands. These facts alone demonstrate the weakness in our quest to develop our unique civilization; for if we weaken our faith, we are at the same time weakening our foundation on which our morality stands. And once we lose that foundation, we'll find ourselves being relegated down to our basic instincts of survival—produce, consume, and die—a formula for survival but not for civilizing.

The dynamics of a civilization consists of two double contrary forces/tendencies and their final outcomes/resultants: The first set of contraries is a resultant of our need of/for stability and permanency—the existence of an unmovable center. The opposite to this requirement is the desire for change—the hope for a better world—which requires the existence and the application of new-dynamic force/energy,—to challenge and affect the current order of things. The second set of contraries emanates from necessity—man to restrain and guide the actions of the heartless, while preserving the individual's independence and motivation to be a creative and valuable member to the collective whole. These individual actions are viewed in respect to the requirements of the social totality—where the single individual can easily be lost, forgotten or both—where the collective size, will, and action(s) are vast, powerful, and absolute, overwhelming its own contrary counterpart. Given these natural disintegrating forces as a fact of human existence, it becomes imperatively necessary—as a civilizing a priori condition—to unify these forces into a balanced whole, in order to establish the required basis for the realization of a continuously evolving, stable civilization in which the four categories of means are sufficient, balanced and applied in an efficient and effective way—where no one category, singularly, dominates and controls the other categories of means, nor where the others, collectively, dominate and control a single category of the means.

The four categories of means/pillars that constitute and are responsible for the creation and the progressive development of a civilization are:

First: The state of governance—must be so directed that its actions must promote/encourage, rather than stifle, creative energy, for it is a central pillar that holds and controls the collective power and energy.

Second: The state of cultural activities—such activities must operate in total freedom, encouraged, promoted, and protected by the state, for it is the pillar that represents and is the flowering of the human spirit, and is its creative force and collective pride!

Third: The state of commercial enterprise—the country's commercial status and condition determines its economic well-being and constitutes its blood vessels, is responsible for the creation and distribution of the wealth of the nation, and sustains and promotes human, scientific, artistic, intellectual, and technical advancement.

Fourth: The state of its religious beliefs—which determines society's spiritual vibrancy and its potency, to connect man to the highest immovable center, and allows him to hope for salvation and divine grace!

Civilizations have divine relativity, but they are not divinely inspired, nor are they divinely ordained; they are man-created and man-determined and are driven by the will of man. They represent and reflect man's aspirations, achievements, as well as his failures. And since by nature man's environment/surroundings are finite, his civilizations must also be finite—i.e., they, like man himself, are created, grow, decline, and eventually will die.

Vibrant and long-lasting civilizations require that they, at their nascent stage, are founded on solid and enduring ground—a vision, a quest, for the unreachable star. It is as the Egyptians did—a quest for man's immortality—around which they created a pantheon of universal gods, and made their king—the pharaoh—a god (the sun god), a supreme and absolute ruler. These universal gods had earthy functions, involved practically in all aspects of man's activities, including his physical body itself. High priests, who surrounded the pharaoh, catered to all of his wishes—his ceremonial duties on this earth; preparations for the pharaoh's journey into the heavens, where he would join and live in eternity with his brother gods. An entire culture developed around the idea of eternity: from the world of the living—the Nile, as the source of life—the pharaohs glorified and remembered by time, with the unsurpassed temples at Karnak, Luxor, Western Thebes, etc.

The world of the dead, their tombs—the pyramids/the house of eternity—are a mystery to us, even at this present day—their purpose still yet unclear, possibly/likely the interim resting place for the embalmed body, waiting for its departed soul to be reunited in perfect bliss for eternity, if —Osiris—god of the underworld—judges that your heart is truthful and your soul is pure. The Egyptians believed in perfect universal order, where everything was in balance and harmony—a state of perfection, fixed and constant, resting on the unmovable Center—the God creator. They saw being/existence as a continuous process of becoming—as part of the cosmic order—from the physical to the spiritual realms of existence, both existing in their own individual identities— one finite, the other infinite—where the finite is infused into the infinite. Man is at one and the same time in heaven and on earth as well. There is—exists a mystical KA—the "immortal" universal spirit, part of which resides in each one of us (an idea that appeared in the Christian doctrine as the Holy Spirit millenniums later).

According to Lionel Casson (*Ancient Egypt*), the Egyptians' "beliefs are not solely reflections of mythical imaginations but involve articulate intelligence and will" behind their explanation of the cause of the act of creation. Ptah "conceived the idea of the universe and executed that idea by uttering a command." The designed creation implies that there is a purpose for each creation, whereby all acting separately—doing their predetermined roles—will in totality fulfill the universal design. The prime mover—the first principle—is the divine God, the chief God—the creator of all. It is in this cosmic order and purpose that the Egyptians sought to fit their own existence; where they designed a sociopolitical structure that emulated the universal system of order and purpose. They made their king, the pharaoh, a god, brother of the gods, to create the immovable center on Earth, establishing a total—absolute—and unquestionable authority in the person of the pharaoh. It is in this way that they established and justified their legitimacy of governance. The question of legitimate succession was a more difficult issue; in case the reigning pharaoh had no son, what then? To resolve this difficult dilemma, they reached all the way up to the chief God and assigned the responsibility to him to produce the needed "heir at law" by requiring him to sleep with the pharaoh's queen. Thus, they ensured a legitimate succession and by a divine, "immaculate" conception: Egyptians held that the gods created a universe "precisely in the form they wanted. Everything therefore was just as it should be—fixed, eternal and proper."

The issues of legitimacy to rule and the heir at law principle reflect society's class structure and its antagonistic reality between the ruling/elite class and the common class—the people—that is, the will of the divine vs. the will of the people. History shows that the will of the divine/dictators prevailed—even today, most of the world is ruled by ruthless, power-hungry dictators, giving themselves—on the basis of might is right—the right to rule without the consent of the people nor a divine blessing. Democracy—the peoples' right to choose their own rulers—is relatively a new ideology, handed down to us by the Greeks, that has established deep roots only in a very limited number of countries, where the will of the people determines the "ruling elite." The problem of democracy, however, is that it is very divisive, cumbersome—slow—ideology-driven, causing confusion and uncertainties in—the long-run—policy matters. It is uncertain as to which path to take to ensure balance and harmony between the well-being of the individual and the public interest—follow the competitive, private ownership and control of the economic means or follow the cooperative, public ownership and control of the same means, or perhaps a mix of the two! Probably, its worst defect stems from its foundation—it rests on an unresolvable paradox, its principle of equal participation, one person, one vote, a rule that leads to a paradox between fairness of representation and responsibility of contribution to the needs of the collective whole. Contribution is done by the "creative few," while equality is enjoyed by the masses, and yet it is the masses who decide who is to rule! Out of this right to equal participation in the political arena arises a transference argument, which maintains that since we are all equal in the political domain, we ought to be equal in all other domains, especially in the wealth domain—hence, and therefore, we all must enjoy the same/ equal standard of living, regardless of effort/sacrifice made—the birth of entitlement—the creation of the welfare state. A program that was meant to help those in need on a temporary basis, giving them a chance to get back on their feet, turned into an entrapment of the very same people that it was helping to get better, into a lifelong (in some cases generational) dependency on the government dole to survive without "any" chance of escaping such ill-designed fate.

In their early dynasties, the Egyptians developed/evolved with an ethical sense of right and wrong—a system of justice—a belief that after life you'll be judged, and judged on the basis of your truthfulness—i.e., the purity of heart and pure conscience. Osiris—the god of the dead—presides over an elaborate trial to determine your fate after death, whether you'll go to eternal life of bliss or you shall be devoured by the hybrid monster. The trial is held in the "Hall of Double Justice," where, on one side of the scale of justice, the heart of the deceased is placed, and on the other side Maat—the goddess of truth and justice—herself or her ideogram, the ostrich feather, is placed. There are also forty-two judges present—representing each province, sitting in judgment of the deceased (equivalent of today's trial by jury). If the scales are in perfect equilibrium, then Osiris will render a judgment of free passage into the Kingdom of Osiris, to live with the gods and the spirits of the dead in eternal bliss. Christian theology adheres to a similar trial, only it is Christ-the-Lord of the universe who sits in judgment. The difference is that if you are found guilty, you are condemned to "live" in hell for eternity; and, of course, the innocent go to heaven, to live in bliss forever, in God's kingdom!

Another similarity between Egyptian mythology and Christian theology is the belief in and the understanding of the trinity doctrine —a situation where three different entities are united into one—Christian trinity consists of the Father/God, the Son/Christ and the Holy Spirit. Larousse Encyclopedia makes at least two references to the idea of trinity: God, Osiris—the fourth divine pharaoh was killed by his brother out of jealousy, was resurrected by his faithful and beloved wife, Isis, and their son, Horus—constituted the "divine" trinity. The other instance of trinity refers to Ptah, the sovereign god of Memphis, Sekhmet—his wife—the beloved of Ptah and his adopted son, Imhotep, formed the "divine" Triad during King Zoser's third dynasty (2686-

1613). "It was claimed that Imhotep was born not of human parents but of Ptah himself."

Let us view and examine the above Egyptian mythical creations and events—in totality—: their obsession with immortality,—life-in-bliss, after death; divine creation; where mortals are elevated to divinity; resurrection of the dead; divine justice to determine purity of the heart and the conscience of man's soul; and perhaps the most significant issue of who or what constitutes the highest universal power and the creator of all—the concept of trinity!

To us today, the above concepts, ideas, and beliefs constitute and represent distant antiquity; they are the Egyptian body of knowledge that we term as mythology. But if we take the same body of knowledge today and applied it to our Christian faith, we identify it as theology. Christianity, in fact, deals with the same body of knowledge as summarized above, with the exception that it chose monotheism—one God vs. polytheism, which the Egyptians believed in. The Egyptians, in fact, did believe in one "chief God"—the creator of "all"—as well as the sub-gods to help him rule the universe; as Christ had his twelve apostles!

The historical "transformation" from mythology to theology occurred in 325, when Constantine I was forced to convene and head the First Ecumenical-Universal-Council to establish some form of uniformity to the young faith, which was more of a movement in disarray and disorder; a movement that was led by Jesus, with a purpose to reform the Jewish faith—on the basis of his teachings. However, with the crucifixion/resurrection of Christ Jesus, and thanks to St. Paul, that movement turned into a deliberate, determined spiritual journey. St. Paul transported and spread Jesus's word of love, salvation and grace to the Gentiles. St. Paul travelled extensively into the Middle East, the Balkans and visited Rome four times. It is due to his efforts that Jesus's word took roots, grew, and turned into a force of faith—pure, innocent, dedicated, and fearless force—withstood and eventually conquered the Roman cruelty, oppression, and murder, but was leaderless and disoriented. Its transformation from a movement to an institutionalized faith—the establishment of a United Universal Church—was extremely difficult, given the fact that it was in and under a Roman Empire and its emperor, who believed himself to be the absolute lord of the world—the earthy Pantocrator—whereby he considered the Christian affairs as only one of the departments of his governing structure. The movement was leaderless and unsure of its fundamental—core—beliefs— i.e., lack of a coherent Christian doctrine. It was for this reason that the Great Ecumenical Council was convened (as explained before) to attempt to establish the needed common core beliefs in the form of doctrinaire tenets.

The deliberations, in essence, centered on the crucial question of the true nature of Jesus. Arius—priest of Alexandria—argued (as stated above) that Jesus was neither eternal nor equal with God, the Father. Athanasius—patriarch of Alexandria and doctor of the Church—vigorously opposed Arius, arguing that Jesus was one with the Father—begotten…being of one essence with the Father. This view prevailed and was issued as a basic creed for all Christians. Thus, the first Ecumenical Council of Nicaea in 325 established the Christian trinity doctrine, made up of the Father, the Son and the Holy Spirit. Here, we have a "Universal Council" made up of 218 Bishops, led by a patriarch, doctor of the Church, headed by a Roman emperor, deciding who is divine—a mortal man determines and proclaims the divine! On what basis and on what precedent? The basis and the precedent are both from past human experience—its reality and mythology were known to the Christian theologians—they simply adopted and transformed the old into the new faith. There but exists a fine line between myth and faith; the universal faiths that we take as "infallible truths" are, in fact, based on and are derived from ancient/antiquity myths. Faith and myth are intertwined; they are both the creation of our fears and hopes—our imagination, perception, and intuition at work! In either case, they serve as the motivating and moving force for the evolvement and the development of our respective civilizations.

The Ancient Greeks—Hellas—and the Romans in essence and method followed—were "in-step with"—the Egyptian model of civilizing. The Greeks, however, differed from the Egyptians in their purpose—which was beauty above all. Their quest for and worship of beauty caused the development of unparalleled architectural marvels; their love for wisdom—logic and reason— led to the development of higher learning institutes, where the masters of philosophy led their students on a journey of discovery of the truth—the concept of justice, the very nature and essence of man himself; the advancement of the arts and literature; unlike the Egyptians—who saw eternity in the universe— they saw a universal idea, universal spirit, universal forces that caused and moved the universe itself—the idea of duality—cause-effect dynamics, order in disorder; kept their gods close to themselves—gave them a place of residence on the top of Mt. Olympus—interacted with them on a human as well as divine level. They left to posterity the richest legacy in the history of man—in thought, reason, word, belief, and in the greatness of man. The age of Renaissance is, in fact, the rebirth of Greek culture, which enabled the West to develop and enjoy an advanced civilization—the fruits that it brings with it! The greatest gift that the Greeks gave to the world is not the Trojan Horse but a new idea of how best to govern ourselves—the idea of democracy—government by the people—the proposition that holds that it is the peoples' inherent right not only to be free but to have the right to participate in the selection process of those that will govern them! A new, novel, and revolutionary idea, reflecting a period of God's chosen—absolute—rulers and society comprised of antagonistic social classes, etc.—but they planted the seed and the seed grew—and we are now reaping the harvest—a harvest of freedom, equal rights—a harvest of human dignity.

Democracy is not an easy nor inspiring form of government; it is based on trust and majority rule, which are difficult to accept completely—especially for the losers—it seems it deals with numbers and counting numbers, rather than the well-being of the people. Democracy as a political system attempts to satisfy Aristotle's axiom—that moderation is the golden rule—neither too much nor too little. That is, as the democratic process works itself out, in that very action, we are cleansing the system of the impurity(ies) of the extremes and thus we are left with the best possible results—i.e., that the best possible results are found in the middle of the political spectrum, where the majority of the people reside. The question is, are the two concepts—the majority and the medium—one and the same thing or are they different; representing entirely different proposi- tions—majority represents numerical—abstract—concept/results, whereas the golden mean represents a qualitative standard—hence, majority rule cannot and does not represent the "best" political results. The belief that extremes are always detrimental to peoples' well-being is not well founded, since it is the extreme policies—once adopted—that become most advantageous/popular to the people, e.g., F.D. Roosevelt and R. Reagan's revolutions; putting aside the rational for equality of participation and the ability of the average voter to be able to select the "best" political results, we can say with certainty that democ- racy is people-friendly and is the foundation—the rock—on which free men stand firm!

Rome—the glory of Rome. The greatest empire that ever existed was based on the belief that Rome was destined for greatness, and to fulfill that destiny, the use of power to subjugate others was justified. This unshakable belief in their greatness, gave the Romans the quest for the unreachable star. This objective motivated the Romans to prove that they were, indeed, great; they created an empire—indeed two empires—lasting more than two millenniums, overcoming enormous difficulties and obstacles, arising from external, as well as, internal forces:

One—Rome's social class structure consisted of—in effect—two classes: the patricians, the nobles, the ruling elite, the Aristocrats, and the land and slave owners. Opposite to the elite class, was the class of common people, the plebeians—of low birth and station. The two classes had nothing in common and shared no common values nor purpose, except that they all were Romans. They, in fact, were the antithesis to each other, and this made them protagonists to one another. This inner struggle pushed and propelled Rome to grow from a small kingdom to a considerable republic and then to a great empire. It is, however, the republic that was dearest to the Roman hearts, because it recognized the people as human beings and the power rested in the hands of the senators—the senate!

Two—As Rome was sliding into a state of imperium, the Republican system of government was not sufficient enough to accommodate the needs of the new empire; it required a greater centralized power base—concentrated in one person—realizing a greater reach; a greater projection; and a greater coordination of power and purpose. This required the building of roads, ships, etc., for faster and more secure transportation of military and commercial ventures—as the Mediterranean Sea became encircled by Roman land forces, in fact, making it the Roman Lake.
Empires require strong and determined hands to lead and rule the expanding empire. Rome never could establish a lasting formula to ensure the empire's succession policy. In case of an emperor's death, many contenders appeared, each claiming the right to succession; it was settled in the field of battle, where the victor got the crown—at the end, the crown was worth nothing—it was offered for sale!

Three—Rome, with its Aristocratic attitude and the pride in the Pax Romana citizenship, developed a superiority vs. inferiority attitude and behavior toward its northern and western neighbors—seeing them as wild Barbarians—uncivilized creatures; which made it impossible for Rome to devise a sound, practical policy to live in peace with them. It, in fact, chose a policy of subjugation by conquest of superior force, a struggle that lasted for centuries and ended disastrously for Rome. The Barbarians, in 410, sacked Rome; King Alaric of the Visigoths—in 419—founded a kingdom in Gaul; in 455 the Vandals sacked Rome; and in 476, Odoacer—Germanic chieftain— deposed the last Western emperor of Rome and effectively put an end to the empire—(*Great Ages of Man: Imperial Rome*, chronology). After their conversion to Christianity, the Barbarians created marvelous Christian states, but misguidedly they misapplied their economic and military power to attack and destroy their sister Christian Church—the Orthodox Christians—by destroying the Byzantine Empire.

In 313, Constantine the Great granted toleration of Christianity, and in 330, forced to abandon Rome as the capital of the empire, he built Constantinople, the new capital of the de facto "new" Roman Empire—the Eastern Roman Empire or the Byzantium. The two Roman Empires were permanently divided in 395 and were never to be united again! With these major changes, the old Pax Romana began to disappear and the new Europa began to emerge—but emerge in an entirely different form, energy and spirit.

Constantine was fashioning his new capital and strengthening the Eastern front, with the hope that the day will come when the East will free the west; the west, however, did not wait for that day; it began to formulate its own future—build on the "unity" of very unlike partners. The foundation was the old Roman structure/infrastructure and their well-known justice system; complemented and supported by the pure Christian moral ethics and divine spirit—applying a well-reasoned attitude toward the Barbarians—and by converting them to the new Christian faith. It accepted them as equal members of the universal church. Moreover, the church showed a profound understanding of the Barbarian character—their free and independent spirit could never be fettered, because if it was, it would die—thus, it chose to follow the principle of separation of church and state. That is, affairs dealing/concerning religious and/or spiritual matters would be the responsibility of the church, headed by the Chief Pontiff—now, the pope. Whereas matters dealing with temporal/ secular issues should be the responsibility of the state—headed by a sovereign ruler—the king. However, the church insisted on two conditions—respecting the above principle: first, Church services must be conducted in Latin; second, all kings must be anointed/crowned by the pontifex maximus—the pope. This unlikely alliance of the three sectors—bringing together the "old" foundation, the new energy and the new vibrant spirit—laid the basis for the creation of the new Europe.

This arrangement initially suited everybody: the church got its independence from the state (unlike the Christian Orthodoxy in the East) to await the second coming of Christ the Lord—concentrate on saving souls rather than acquiring worldly riches. It had the power of coronation as well as the power of holy baptism; enjoyed a vindication satisfaction over the "old" Roman oppressors; and spiritually, it held the key to the doors of heaven! The Barbarians were Christians, became the spirit-men—an elevation from the "almost" animal status—were independent to pursue the development of their own states. As far as the old Rome was concerned, it had to adapt to the new reality—they became very useful in the administrative affairs of the state. With time, the old dies, the new takes over—ushering in new ideas; new views; new desires; new ambitions, greed takes over, driving a wedge between church and state; the temptation for worldly wealth was irresistible—for it represented power, influence, control, prestige, and respect, while the church represented and offered something intangible, uncertain, a world unknown—a spirit world; required that we live our earthy lives according to the requirements of that world—Christ-like life—which, as humans, we are incapable of doing—we fear the day of judgment because we doubt our own purity of heart and soul!

The triple alliance became an uneasy rivalry between church and state—each claimed superiority/preeminence over the other; rivalry and jealousy set in among states; new state alliances formed and reformed, the church guided/manipulated most. It even reconstituted the Old Roman Glory, with its own Christian cross—the Holy Roman Empire—in the name of Charlemagne— Charles the Great—the emperor of the West; King of the Franks (768-814); King of the Lombards, conqueror of northeast Spain; subjugated and Christianized the Saxons (772-804); defeated the Avars and the Wends. In 800, he restored Leo III to the Papal See; in gratitude, the Pope—Leo III—crowned him the emperor of the "new" Roman Empire—the Holy Roman Empire—on Christmas Day in Rome. This coronation—in gratitude and at the same time deliberate—laid the basis for a permanent division and separation between the two Christian universal churches. This event, in effect, was a direct and deliberate challenge not only to the Christian Orthodox Church but even more so to the emperor of the Eastern Roman Empire—Constantine VII—as the head of state, as the Roman emperor of the entire Roman Empire, as well as the head of the Christian Church. With a single coronation, Pope Leo III and King Charles, revolted against the inherited preeminent position held by the Eastern Roman emperor since Constantine I—both as emperor and the titular head of the Christian Church—and claimed the two titles for themselves!

The Eastern Roman Empire followed the Roman tradition of governance, continued by Constantine I (330), based on the imitation of how the universe is ruled—one Lord of the universe, one emperor on Earth—both secular as well as spiritual matters were/must be under one emperor. This formula fitted—quite nicely—the Christian doctrine—Christ, the Pantocrator—the Lord of the universe—hence, the emperor—Lord of the world. The timing of the revolt was perfect; the ambitious Irene—the co-emperor with her son, Constantine VII—proclaimed herself as the sole emperor/empress of the Eastern Roman Empire after she blinded her son. Pope Leo III proclaimed the Byzantine throne vacant, since Irene was a woman and the throne must be occupied by a male—a precedent established by the twelve apostles—all being male. Pope Leo III, with a single coronation, not only usurped the Byzantine crown but also declared that the pope—i.e., himself—was the head of all Christendom—he, in fact, assumed primacy in all spiritual affairs over the Eastern Roman Empire. This masterful plot failed because in Constantinople, the palace revolted against Irene and proclaimed Nicephorous as emperor. The west was relentless in its drive to subsume the Byzantine Empire and its Orthodox Church under their control. Another contentious issue arose when St. Ignatius—patriarch of Constantinople—lost his position; a Greek theologian was ordained to take his place (858); Pope Nicholas I, however, refused to recognize him as the legitimate patriarch of Constantinople, because of his contrary position to the Roman See on the issue of Iconoclasm. Photinus responded by calling the Synod to question and evaluate some Latin beliefs/customs—in particular, the pope's right to pass judgment on the election of Byzantine patriarchs. This schism marked the beginning of the end, the split between the two Christian universal churches. And in 1054, the Byzantine Church broke with the Roman See.

There was an important, ongoing disagreement concerning a doctrinarian issue—dealing with the "proper" relationship between the Son and the Holy Spirit in the concept of the holy trinity. The Nicaean Ecumenical Council declared that there is a Father/God, the Son and the Holy Spirit—the Son and Spirit emanate from the Father, of course; but the council, specifically, did not proclaim the exact relationship between the Son and the Spirit— the Orthodox Church worked on the inferred premise that the two entities are both holy, unique in their own creation, and separate—they are coequal inhabitants of the holy trinity. The Catholic See took a different position, elevating the Son much more closer to the Father—a divinity who has been with the Father from the beginning of all creation; must have been and has taken part in the creation of the Holy Spirit—hence, the Holy Spirit emanates from both the Father and the Son—that is, the Father and the Son are divine but the spirit is "only" holy! John the Baptist, however, tells us that when Jesus came down on Earth to save mankind, He waited for the Holy Spirit to arrive and "empower" Him to perform baptism; this indicates—clearly—that Jesus did not outrank the Holy Spirit. We should not forget the role of the Holy Spirit in the immaculate conception of Jesus Himself! The difficulty here—as I have argued before—is the concept—the idea—of trinity itself; and more specifically, what do we mean by the idea of the Holy Spirit—is it an extension (tool) of God, to do His bidding, or is it a separate entity, with its own identity, will, and purpose? In Jesus's case, according to John, Jesus tells us that He is on Earth to do God's will, not His own. This defines Jesus as a separate, complete being—the Son of the Father, doing His Father's bidding—a family "without" a mother; the Egyptian trinity did have a mother! At any rate, the disagreement was never resolved.

The question of primacy did not go away; the Roman Catholic Church, in order to justify its rightful claim as the legitimate head of all Christendom and Rome as the universal Center, presented what it calls the Petrine Supremacy Doctrine, which in effect contends that the pope is a direct successor to St. Peter by virtue of Peter's position as the Chief Pontiff of Rome's Church and his cruel death by the Roman Empire in 67. He is referred to as the prince and the leader of the twelve apostles after the crucifixion of Jesus. He is pictured holding the keys of the gates of heaven. Jesus, after his resurrection, charged Peter to "feed my sheep." Here, we see Peter—the rightful successor to Jesus and his mission—and this is exactly what Peter endeavored to do—he ministered north of Jerusalem, Antioch, etc., following in the footsteps of his master—healing, ministering. Peter, the loyal and trusted friend—defending and spreading his master's mission of love and peace and His deeds of conversion to salvation. The emphasis is on Jesus's reform of a corrupt Jewish religion—to transform it—give it love, grace, and salvation—which Peter embraced wholeheartedly and pursued. There was no intent to start nor create a "new" religion—only a serious transformation of the existing one! For this reason, Peter was against the conversion of the Gentiles—because it was a "matter of required circumcision, that was part of the covenant between Moses and His God," which the Gentiles never practiced. St. Peter "changed his mind—late in his life," when he decided to go to Rome. Also, he realized St. Paul's success in the conversion of the Gentiles to Jesus's faith. "This and much more was happening. St. Paul believed himself to be a "new" prophet, charged by God to carry out a mission of transforming Jesus's movement into a faith—transforming Jesus of the gospels into Christ of theology." Durant explains: "Paul had found a dream of Jewish eschatology, confined in Judean Law; he had freed and broadened it into a faith that could move the world...interwove the ethics of the Jews with the metaphysics of the Greeks." A transformation of the personal Jesus Christ to the metaphysical Christ Jesus! Jewish ethics—Moses's rules of conduct—to the "new" level of morality, determined behavior for salvation. The road to Christ Jesus—tells us St. Paul—is in our hands; God has given us free will and a conscience to determine our own fate by the application of that free will tempered/guided by our conscience, to ensure in our struggles between good and evil that the good always prevails—this moral path, at Judgment Day, will ensure our salvation—this faith process rests upon our covenant with God, in a form of our creed!

"In short, St. Peter gives us Jesus, whereas St. Paul gives us Christ—the Son of God!"

It amazes and saddens me to learn that neither the West nor the East has given St. Paul the credit and recognition that he deserves for creating a faith—with a theological foundation on which it still stands, but also a faith that gives its followers a hope for eternal life; but for more than one hundred years, the two Christian Churches forgot that he even existed; they were too busy—in their own ways—devising means to justify their own preeminence over the other, forgetting the real issue/essence of the faith itself.

The two apostles of Christ were competitors/rivals trying to spread the Lord's message in their own way, but above all they were brothers in Christ and true believers in His God—the Father. It is this Christian brotherhood that the two churches failed to adhere to that caused the rift between them, and that rift dragged in the two apostles, on opposite sides. It was a fundamental error in judgment that the West Christian Church chose to use St. Peter as a tool to justify its preeminence status—the Petrine Supremacy Doctrine—to impose its will and dictates to its sister Church. In view of the above analysis, one can make an indisputable case for a Paulene Preeminence Principle—based on religious grounds—his creation of a new Christian faith, rather than on distant precedent and on great wealth and military might. If Paul had been given his due recognition—a long time ago—the world today would be much different, and probably for the better.

The center for Christian activities would—most likely—have been Ephesus, in Asia Minor; Paul's center of operations united East and West in the center. Certainly, Rome and Constantinople were wrong and the most unsuitable locations for the evolvement and the development of a new, pure, innocent and full-of-hope faith. Both, in essence and in spirit, were not only influenced but determined by the forces of the old and the "new" Roman imperium; and by the subsequent wrong choices that each in turn made. I am confident that if Ephesus had become the center of Christian activity of worship, there would not have existed rivalry between the East and the West, since there would have been no reason for it—the center would have united East and West in faith, socially, economically, and politically. The sociopolitical union would have been strong enough to repulse any Ottoman Turkish invasion. The need for crusades would not have existed, but as it is, the fourth crusade invaded, destroyed, and conquered Constantinople—established the Latin Empire to replace the Byzantine Empire—did not last long—the crusades failed completely in their mission to free Jerusalem. This adventure weakened the Byzantine Empire— what was left of it—enabling the Ottoman Turks to overwhelm the Balkan states—piecemeal—one by one, until they reached the gates of Vienna in 1529. The Western powers did not come to the aid of the struggling Balkan states; they were conquered and enslaved by the Turks for over 500 years—erasing all traces of their national identities and arrested their natural aspirations and their cultural and economic development through the entire Balkan region, leaving ugly consequences that are, even today, haunting the Balkan people.

These ventures established a pattern of conquests—imperialism—based on economic grounds/interest and the use of force as the justifiable means toward an end. It's a principle that eventually led to two disastrous wars—WWI and WWII—destroying most of the Christian world, and for what?—for preeminence and predominance over others!

Dr. Toynbee recognizes the two Christendoms as two of the major civilizations that ever existed in the history of the world. The conclusion is too generous and is not supported by historical deeds, especially as applied to the West Christendom. With the advent of technology and discoveries of a scientific nature—their applications created different states, which emerged after the collapse of the Roman Empire, leaving Europe without a center of power that would hold them together—the church failed; new city-states grew in power and predominance, propelling them to new adventures and conquests of foreign lands in the name of Christianity—God's gift of free will was taken as unfettered freedom to amass worldly material possession; God's second gift— the conscience, the restraining force to man's unlimited greed—was totally ignored; in fact, being rich is a mark of success, a standard of progressivity!

This delusionary quest for an attachment to material possessions, coupled with the failure of the church to properly guide the believers to seek spiritual enlightenment, created/resulted in the deficiency of and in our faith in God. We have allowed the earthy reality—the needs of the flesh—to precede and overwhelm our spirit reality; this material domination eclipses our cultural, as well as our spiritual, developments; without the existence of both, we cannot build the required foundation on which we stand firm—with pride and dignity, surrounded by nature's beauty, man's goodness and innocence and God's grace—only then can we claim that we are civilized. The Greeks and, to a lesser extent, the Egyptians did it. WHY CAN'T WE?

PART III
CAPITALISM—ITS ETHICAL AND MORAL DILEMMA

Economics deals with essentials for the survival of the human race; it examines the principle of Scarcity, which represents the relationship between the means and the ends—that is, the productive resources at our disposal and our needs and wants that "must" be satisfied. The principle of scarcity holds that human needs and wants are urgent, variable, increasing and are in fact unlimited; whereas the means are scarce, limited in versatility, quality and quantities, exhaustible and finite.

This relationship between the unlimited human desires and the limited means—natural as well as human—represents the infinite ceaselessly pushing, clashing with tremendous force, demanding their dreams and hopes be realized; against the finite world of limitations, shortages and insufficiencies of goods and services that are needs and wants satisfiable. This stress/tension represents and constitutes the law of scarcity—the basis/foundation of the field of economics.

As the means of production change, the mode of production undergoes a corresponding change, facilitating the production of new induced demand for the now available new goods and services—increasing the appetites for the consumers' needs and wants, thereby causing the economic problem of scarcity to expand, once again validating the law of scarcity—the definition of economics.

Simply stated, man's infinite needs, wants and desires—due to his egocentric nature—cannot be met/satisfied by the finite resources of the world. The catastrophe will come when the finite is exhausted to the point where there are no new resources to be found and the existing resources are insufficient/unable to feed the ever-increasing world population. The idea that existence in certain areas of the world possessing relative affluence renders the scarcity principle null and void and thus irrelevant is misleading and wrong. Today, the world of 7.5 billion people, to reach and enjoy the American standard of living of about forty-eight thousand dollars per capita, will need to provide a global GDP of about $360 trillion, a deficiency of $240 trillion—equal to thirty-two thousand dollars per capita; that is, we'll need to increase our global production, without any population increases, by two-thirds of current production—an absolute impossibility!

There is really no such thing as a wholly satisfied, fully affluent person; the desire for more is always there and grows with time, because the new is always better—in fashion—preferable to the old. We may romanticize the old—talk about it in glowing and glorious terms—because we are talking about our parents/grandparents, their heroes—the best of the human race—but, at the same time, we rebel against their way of life; we create and embrace our own way simply because it is ours, it represents our sacrifices and achievements—affluence has nothing to do with it!

The greatest motivating factor for that drive is our nature—the inherent/inner motive of the imperative of our differentiation in which we find and enjoy distinction, uniqueness, and pride in our individual achievements. It is in this that we find meaning and purpose in life; it is not to be found in uniformity, equality, and sameness, where the individual is de-individualized and depersonalized by the collective weight. It is in that imperative of differentiation that our progress resides—it is the foundation for our different skills, experiences, capabilities, and competencies, which we are able to demonstrate and apply in our lives to ensure the greatest possible outcomes/results of goods and services.

The trend of ever-increasing public assistance programs inevitably leads to the condition of sameness and equality, which is in contradiction to the above proposition. They are in the long run detrimental to the recipients themselves, because they become dependent on the collective ideology—losing their independence and, thereby, their individuality, which will hinder them and rob them of their ability to pursue their own ambitions, desires, hopes and dreams—and by their realizations, will feel pride and fulfillment as useful and valuable members of the community/society. Their social dependency will instill in them a separate value system, which is not of their making but the making of the collective, artificially created environment of which they have no control whatsoever. In order to justify their social dependency, preserving their inherent pride as human beings, they fall on the explanation that it is the unfortunate circumstance that brought them to where they are today. This, then, is the excuse and justification for not only receiving social assistance but for claiming that they are entitled to it—hence the claim to the ownership thereof! It is a rationalization based on the socialistic ideology that claims the existence of a collective umbrella that protects all of its citizens—equally, no matter who or what they are or what they are doing or not doing—it is the membership of the collective that is the a priori condition needed to qualify for social benefits. We are all brothers and sisters, and as such we are all equal in the eyes of the collective conscience—all unions embrace this premise. Christianity is also based on this principle—we are all equal in the eyes of God! Democracy also is based on this principle of equality—one person, one vote. It is from these three areas of the acceptance of the equality principle that we may/can infer that it ought to apply to our economic system as well. Hence, all of our wealth and income must be distributed equally; hence, the idea of redistribution was born, embraced and is in style today. The inference principle of the application of the equality principle is not applicable to the area of Economic Wealth, since the previous three examples of equality and its application carry no losses of sacrifices that are punishing those that created/produced that wealth/income; and by confiscating it from its rightful owner—the differentiated individuals—you are destroying the very foundation that nurtures the motive and the inner urge to create and excel through hard work, sacrifices, and risk!

The question is not whether we should help those less fortunate and in need, for whatever reason; rather, it is how best to do it? The collective assistance methods, such as welfare and all the others that constitute the safety net for the poor, are not successful at all. The same problems still exist and are increasing—some are even transferable from one generation to the next. We cannot solve the problem of poverty by simply expending and extending the same programs without affecting and changing the core of the problem. The fundamental state of the problem is that those people—whether due to their own actions or inactions or whether their problems are caused by external forces beyond their control—are not useful to the productive/creative process of society; they live and breathe at the margins of the social fabric—they are the invisible among us—we simply do not see them, except during elections, but only for a while. The real issue is, how do we make them visible all the time? Simply by making them useful all the time! It is by their full integration into the society, as full—creative/useful—members of that society. To achieve this full integration, we must help them acquire valuable/useful skills, knowledge, behavior, and attitudes that are needed and valued by the society in order to qualify for the full integration/incorporation in that very society. Two examples that I know might help us; what is at issue—what is our role and what is their role, and our obligations?: the first example deals with two neighbours, getting along well, one technically inclined, the other not so much. The second neighbor has a car problem, the car will not start; asks the first neighbor for help, and he agrees; opens the hood—does something, turns the car key, and the car starts. The second neighbor looks at him is dismay, and says: I did not ask you to start the car, but to show me how it is done so that I can do it myself!

The second example has to do with a poor family and a wealthy landlord living in the same village. The landlord, probably out of pity, wants to help the poor family—not to starve—but does not want to give them ready food, to spare their pride, so he talks to the poor man and makes him an offer; when harvesting the big field of wheat, I'll harvest the field in a circle, leaving the four corners for your family to harvest, so that you will not be hungry; the poor man accepts the kind offer—the family survives.

These two examples demonstrate that we should not only help but, more importantly, it is how we do it that is of great significance. The first example teaches us that there is a fundamental difference between handouts—such as welfare programs—and helping the poor to acquire useful skills, training, education, etc., which will enable them to not only survive but become useful—productive individuals, being part of and belonging to the labour force; and in that capacity, they will compete, perform on an equal basis with the rest of us—and when this happens, the integration is complete!

Social integration, rather than social segregation, will free the poor from the collective dependence and make it possible for them to seek, on their own, meaning and purpose in life, on an equal basis as the rest of us do! It is this goal—the right to be free of dependency—that gives the poor the right to social assistance, which constitutes their justification for that assistance.

Our ethical imperative dictates that we, as free individuals, through our collective conscience, are responsible to ensure that each one of us has a sufficient opportunity to develop his or her capacities/potentialities to the extent that is necessary to earn a decent living, commensurate with his or her own merits. The equivalent moral imperative states that human life is sacred, and its pain and suffering must be alleviated by the collective conscience and actions of giving, as an a priori condition of that sacredness.

This right of "entitlement," however justified, cannot be limitless—it is timely and conditional. The second example teaches us that the recipients of public assistance must accept corresponding measures of responsibilities, on their own, for their own lives, by doing their part in the process of their social integration; they must be diligent, hard-working—go to school, study hard, and succeed—this requirement is not an option—it is a binding agreement; exceptions are illnesses and children of minority age, which will be accommodated with flexible programs. The flexibility programs shall extend and cover cases where the recipients, after successful completion of their training, cannot find work; the National Employment Agency shall find for such cases, in-training places of work for one year; if that fails to secure full-time employment for the recipient/candidate, then the employment agency—with full power of the law—shall find and place the candidate either in the public or private sector as a full employee, commensurate with his or her merits. The private sector cannot refuse such a responsibility—since it is a small measure of repayment for getting a free, trained, educated labour force at public expense; and, of course, other useful considerations as well.

It is only if we look at this problem in this way, where we are obligated, either individually or collectively, to ensure that each one of us has a sufficient enough opportunity to develop his or her skills/education to the extent that is required for earning a decent living, that it will give us the common ground on which we can establish the basis for our ethical and moral responsibility to our fellow men. It is not the idea of entitlement, nor is it our duty or a sense of equality or fairness that is the justification for such assistance; it is, however, the sense of our obligation toward each other as human beings that is the key in unlocking the mystery of poverty that establishes the moral imperative for action. If we are all well and secure, the collective whole will also be well and strong!

Inequality has existed since the creation of mankind; wealth and power are elusive commodities—affluent today, poor tomorrow; they shift—irrespective of loyalty—with the uncertain socioeconomic winds; creating new means and new needs, which lead to the creation of a new mode of production—a new economic system; that, in time, will come in conflict with the current ethical values; and this, in turn, will spill over into the sphere of our sense of morality. Coping and adjusting to these shifting epochs of change constitutes our life's endeavors, forcing upon us the need to adapt, individually as well as collectively; whereby, due to our state of differentiation, some will rise to the challenge(s) of change and do well, others will be crushed by its weight and will fall—the reversal of fortunes will occur!

The economic imperative of survival—the needs of the flesh caused, and continue to cause, a great deal of difficulties to the Christian morality, whose prime concern was/is the eternal salvation of the soul of man. Jesus Christ himself chased the money lenders from the temple as being evil in their deeds, practicing usury; it did not do much good—our banks today are doing the same thing—they give you 1.6 percent for your term deposits, but they charge you 23 percent on your Visa balance, a difference of 21.4 percent—a perfect example of usury!

Christianity has wrestled unceasingly, ever since its beginning, with the dilemma of precedence between the flesh and the soul. The soul, of course, holds predominance; however, the home of the homeless soul is the body of the man; and to save the soul, you must feed the body—the flesh!

Constantine I, the emperor of the Byzantine Empire, faced this very dilemma in 330—known as the Monastic Succession—a fundamental theological issue surfaced, threatening the Christian unity. The issue, simply, was about which way forward Christians? As the Christians sought converts, they interacted with others possessing different values and attitudes. These two-way interactions not only influenced the others; but they in turn influenced the Christians as well. The interactions, especially with the wealthy, presented an irresistible temptation to the Christians for worldly goods, which represented the good life on this earth. Many succumbed and became wealthy themselves in their own right. This tendency toward affluence by the faithful gained strength and spread rapidly; an occurrence that went against the main teaching of Christ Himself: that God is a spirit and the spirit above gives life; the flesh is of no significance; the ceremony of baptism guarantees eternal life. To serve God through Christ, you must reject worldly possessions and pleasures; they are egotistic and evil; devote yourself to purely spiritual pursuits—contemplation in thought and eternal life! The minority, according to Durant, who sought to be true to the original Christian beliefs withdrew from the Church—splitting the Church into two factions. Constantine, as well as the Church, could not tolerate such a division and put an end to it—Constantine for political reasons, and the Church for theological ones; the Church was not sure that the path of contemplation and isolation was the right path to follow, since detachment led to the negation of man—it nullifies love for one another, a complete rejection of Christ's basic and fundamental tenet. This the Church could not accept as a valid alternative—Christ as the true and only path was reaffirmed.

This reaffirmation, however, was loaded with unforeseen consequences that we are still struggling with to this very day; since "Christ is the path" did/does not resolve the social dilemma between affluence and poverty—its ethical and moral implications—Christ's way, it seems, accepted both realities, the reality of affluence and the reality of poverty. Much later on, the Church semi-reversed its position and encouraged the development of monasteries and convents to serve God, but also to be used as a countervailing force against affluence: its greed for material possessions. It did not do much good, since man's inner instincts for preservation of life on this earth proved to be irreconcilable with the Church's mere, abstract promise of eternal salvation of man's soul by mere baptism! The flesh has won the day, because (as stated before) to save the soul, you must feed the man. The soul lost because the rising new faith was not certain of its fundamental doctrines/tenets—there are too many paradoxes and uncertainties in it to assure man that its path to eternal life is the true one! It became obvious that the Church had to bend and accept the inevitable, that if the soul is to reach its eternal salvation place, it had to wait for the flesh to live its allotted time, given to it by no lesser authority—God, Himself.

The issue of monasticism and its aftermath reoriented the debate from a moral point of view to one that deals with survival of man on this earth—i.e., the ethics of survival—the nature of the argument was altered from an in-kind category to an in-degree category, and went as far as maintaining that "thou shalt earn thy bread by the sweat of thy brow," suggesting that economic success is synonymous with the Christian faith; representing self-respect, distinction, social status, proof of one's worth, and virtue. This achievement, value-oriented, Protestant-Puritan approach is an attempt to synthesize the two irreconcilable realities; it places hard-work ethics (affluence achievement) as an a priori condition in respect to the virtues of the soul. The inferred premise here is that a "contented" soul residing in our affluent body has an a priori right to the gates of heaven over all the other tortured souls. With economic progress, and the corresponding increase in the standard of living, the virtue of hard work gained social recognition and acceptance, diminishing religious influence in social affairs. This secularization of religious matters decreased the Church's influence on social interactions, and thereby reducing it as a force, determining human and social behavior on moral grounds. Thus, the moral reigns of restraint were not only totally removed but were perversely used as an ethical instrument to justify corporate behavior of greed, corruption, indifference to individual rights, disregard for the free market system.

The struggle between ethical objectives and the moral imperative—the efforts of reconciliation between ethics and morality—continued on the basis of values as time progressed: on the basis of happiness and individual freedom; then on humanitarian grounds of equality and common justice; then on to freedom—a social value above all others!

We have travelled a long road to get to where we are now over two thousand years later, and we have done many things, good and bad, but these perversions of Jesus's teachings—his sacrifice for us, etc.—represent the highest kind of betrayal that the world has ever witnessed; the gross misrepresentation and degradation of His ideas and His beliefs. We have adopted a convoluted version of His beliefs to suit our convenience and purpose. Moral constraints/restraints do not exist; the hope of salvation is but a transparent hypocrisy—an illusion! The only constraint left is the secular sense of Social Ethics—a collective stand that is based on the proposition that unbridled affluence breeds contempt and indifference for those that are less fortunate. It's an attitude of behavior that leads to the division of society into classes; which in turn creates hatred between the haves and the have-nots—the old Roman classes, the plebeians versus the patricians; that threatens to destroy the very social fabric that holds us all together!

To prevent the destruction of the fabric that binds us together, it is essential that the social classes are brought closer together in a tolerable working balance. The top affluent class must curtail its zeal to amass greater and greater amounts of wealth; and the bottom class must begin to assume greater responsibility for its own existence/life. The current attempts to bridge the great divide between affluence and poverty by redistribution of wealth/income is not a sound policy nor is it a workable solution to this enduring problem; it is, at best, a patchwork of government programs pacifying the poor for a short while. There is no political will to get to the core of the problem of extreme wealth versus extreme poverty. The fundamental cause for these extremes are the government policies that favour the rich and work against the poor, and the flawed social system, its attitudes, conduct, and influence are so ingrained against the poor, as being lazy, drunkards, worthless, irresponsible, and so on. But the attitude toward the rich is one of respect, trust—they can enter the prime minister's office while the others cannot! The affluence not only controls power, but it has an enormous influence over the social fabric; there exists an invisible convergence at the top levels of all the major industrial, governmental, legal, artistic, press, and educational elites that, all together, constitute the ruling class; a class that is a built-in structure of the collective organization, and is an indispensable part of the society. Left-leaning political parties have attempted to break this ingrained social elite without any significant success—they are firmly and invisibly bound and held together by their mutual interests, respect, trust, and uniqueness.

The eradication of poverty is not to be found in the redistribution of our wealth, but in the realignment of the social/legal structures of our society to give the lower class a fair chance to succeed. It must do everything possible to get out of the collective imprisonment, dependency, and moral degradation.
If a business corporation experiences difficulties—due to the CEO's incompetence—it gets bailed out by the government with public funds; a much different treatment than that of a poor family. The reason for this is the fact that businesses are incorporated as legal entities—with all legal entitlements, protection, tax exemptions, hiring workers who are trained/educated at public expense, their private fortunes protected by law, as it is separated from the business, and many other advantages. The CEOs' salaries used to be based and determined

by performance; now, incompetent CEOs are paid hundreds of millions of dollars to leave their jobs. Whatever happened to the free enterprise system, where competition determined who stays in business and who does not! Today, the new thing is groupings—in banks, airlines and so on.

This is a new form of subverting and degrading the free-market process, by agreements between corporations to do joint ventures under the radar of the antitrust regulators; using the excuse that it is necessary to enable them to compete with "bigger" worldwide conglomerates. A logic that, if followed to the nth degree, will leave the world with only two conglomerates—a frightening scenario!

Two cases that will illustrate my concerns: The first deals with the airline industry. For the last sixteen years, I have suffered from rheumatic arthritis and find it necessary to get away from the humidity that overwhelms Toronto during the summers; I go to Eastern Europe, in the Balkans, where it is cooler and dryer. This summer I ended up with the Star Alliance—a grouping between Lufthansa and Air Canada—it seems Lufthansa is in charge of Air Canada's European flights, etc. The way the Star Alliance works is like a shell game; e.g., Air Canada schedules a flight to Frankfurt on a given day and given hour, books the large Airbus hoping to fill it up with passengers. However, before the scheduled flight departs, the airline finds that only 60 percent of the tickets are sold! What to do? The Alliance partner comes to the rescue; it is ready with a smaller plane to take over the flight: it is just about the right size to accommodate Air Canada's 60 percent passengers—the profit margin is now 100 percent. The confirmed seats that we arranged with the Air Canada flight are now null and void; and when we got to the airport to obtain our boarding pass, not only did we not get seats, but the plane left and left us for the next day; the next day, the same shell game repeated—frustration and disappointment, to say the least.

What I really want to point out to the prime minister is not my personal grievance, but what effect(s) such groupings have on our free enterprise system, especially on competition? The two airlines are supposed to be competitors, are they not? After the Star Alliance agreement is in effect, they are no longer competitors but partners! This vertical alliance, in my mind, has adverse, negative effects on our free enterprise system. This is what I wrote to the chairman and CEO of Lufthansa, in my letter of complaint about the hardship, etc., that we endured. "Second, is the economic harm that is due to weakening the foundation of the Free Market System—the degradation of competition, by the creation of greater concentration of wealth/capital in fewer hands—your Star Alliance is a perfect example of such concentration—loss of competition, which, in fact, is unlawful—it is contrary to the Anti-Trust Law, the FTO Commission. You, more than anyone else, certainly know that the Free Enterprise System thrives best when economic power is dispersed, enabling many to compete in a fair and equal basis; this in turn guarantees the most efficient allocation of our scarce resources, and provides us with the best "Economic Standards of Living.""

No reply; the best policy is to ignore the complaint.

The second example deals with the chartered banks; their concentration of power path falls into the category of horizontal alliances with businesses having nothing to do with banking, which is charged with the creation of deposits and dispersal of credits in the financial market. Evidently, on the basis of having a captive clientele, our banks decided to make profitable business by offering their clients out-of-country medical insurance, underwritten by another company, through their VIP Gold Visa credit card. The coverage was quite attractive for us, during the summers, travelling to Eastern Europe. A few years ago, the bank, without any notice, cancelled the coverage for clients sixty-five years old and over—the senior citizens. This move on the part of the bank was very disappointing, since we have been their clients since 1965—Calgary. I wrote a letter to the president, expressing our disappointment; but more importantly the fact that, since they are targeting a group of citizens on the basis of age, who are protected by the charter of our rights and freedoms—Article 15, p. 4—the Constitution Act, 1982—they are in fact committing a discriminatory act.

The reply was the following:

"…while age does play a part in determining costs, the premiums are not based on unfair or unlawful discrimination; rather they are based on probability of claims."
This quote notwithstanding, I still believe that I am right; but more strongly, I believe that bankers have no business selling insurance.

The above two examples illustrate the helplessness of the individual against the almighty corporation, its arrogance and indifference to the helpless individual. If the individual, whether poor or not so poor, is to regain some respect, confidence, and influence, the family, as the core social institution—the creator of the future generation (the labor force)—must be strengthened by legal and financial means. I propose, therefore, that it be given incorporated legal status—equivalent to that of the corporations, enabling it to claim (as the businesses do) all of its family expenses as income tax deductibles and pay income tax only on the net income. The proposal will, of course, have a cutoff point of—let's say—$120,000, or it will be based on a sliding scale. If this comes to pass, the lower class will get a tremendous boost financially, as well as emotionally. The socioeconomic advantages will be to push upward the burden of the income tax to those that benefit most and are able to pay—thus tightening the extreme social groups toward the middle-center, reducing the social stress and increasing social cohesion!

Further to this proposal, we must add two more; the first has to do with provision/access to equal, universal opportunity education and training, all the way up to and including college and university; at least four years of training—BA, BSc., etc.; collectively paid for by the family, the business community, and the public; one-third each. Second: The required social attitudes for integration rather than identification. Those who receive public assistance are labeled by the very nature of that assistance—e.g., rental, low-income housing, food stamps, and so on. This method of assistance identifies the recipients by area and/or by character, as separate beings from the rest of us—these ghettoization and marginalisation ought to be avoided as much as possible. The method of payments for rentals/housing should be made invisible as much as possible, via the banks. In this way, the recipient will put some of his or her money in the same account plus the state's amount, enabling him or her to find on his or her own housing accommodations among us. These ways of providing assistance will go a long way in helping recipients to realize the goal of integration much easier and faster.

If we are to achieve the needed moral imperative, the ethical necessity requires that we reject the view of man as being an animalistic being and as such greedy because he uses his instinct to survive, which is nonsense; in fact, he is a unique human being, possessing intelligence, conscience, and will—created in the image of God. He lives and breathes with the likes of him; in a communal social setting; which establishes their interactions and interrelationship on an individual basis, as well as their collective whole; this, in turn, requires the creation of a set of rules that will determine their behavior and conduct—that are fair for all equally to ensure harmonious existence for all. These rules of conduct consist of a series of actions and reactions among the individuals themselves, and the actions-reactions among the individuals and their social institutions—on the following basis of interactions:

I.   The individual versus the collective whole—resulting in our Happiness Index.

II.   Liberty versus authority—resulting in our Freedom Index.

III. Affluence versus poverty—resulting in our well-being—the Equality Index.

IV.   Right versus wrong—measures the degree of achievement in #III— the Justice Index.

V.   The old versus the new—the past is known and is already judged; the future is unknown and is full of promise/expectation—a hope for a better future—this determines our Progress Index.

VI.   Good versus bad—includes all of our pursuits and endeavours and their achievements and failures—measures our humanism index— the essence of our being.

These are the six social planes of social and personal interactions, with their corresponding ethical values; which, in turn, will determine and reflect our personal and collective achievements, as well as failures—that is, our worth, our virtues and compassion, and our kindness as human beings! These interactions represent our struggles and challenges, creating opportunities for success, but they also constitute constraints and limitations that, if misjudged/misapplied, could lead to catastrophic ends.

To facilitate, accommodate, and protect these interactions, society must establish a social framework of acceptable conduct and behavior by determining the essential boundaries and limitations and their counterparts—our freedoms and our rights, wherein we, as individuals, will be able to think, act, and freely develop our unique characters as ordained by our individual nature and, in time, will evolve with the essence of our being. It will provide, on a collective basis, the essential services to all of its citizens, equally, universally and indivisibly, based on our moral and ethical grounds—their right to security, health, and education; everything else must be left to the individual to deal with according to his or her aspirations, motivation, dreams, and hopes!

Morality deals with the soul—it is an experience of our conscience; the struggle of our inner agony of defeat vs. our inner ecstasy of joy, i.e., the inner struggle between good and evil. Usually it is the organized religions that are the purveyors of morality, simply because they are the saviours of souls. This, however, does not imply nor does it preclude the fact that all human beings possess souls, regardless of their faith or lack thereof. Faith and souls are individual attributes and possessions; and it is how the individual chooses, or is forced to apply them, that constitutes and is the subject of morality. Its purpose is to place man on a higher state of being, by transcending man into the otherworldly, spirit, reality of being, where beauty, grace, and innocence reign supreme! Morality is not, as with ethics, a learned proposition; it is derived by experience—your own sufferings, tragedies, tortures, etc., and by the experiences of others, by projecting oneself into their predicaments, agonies, tortures, and so on, through our inner senses of our conscience.

These experiences will cause us to become more altruistic—less egotistic for fear that such calamity may befall us; this transcendental/transference is not an absolute, but a matter of degrees. It is a protective gesture to avoid harm, like the fear of God's wrath. It is a feeling of sorrow for ourselves through seeing/witnessing it in others. It is an expression and admission of our weaknesses and fallibility as human beings. The strong have no morality because they feel invincible; they have no need of mitigating ethical rules because they are above such constraints; the laws/rules are impositions/irritants; the inner feeling toward the concern for others. The ethical rules can be broken, once the conditions of the social compact are broken, destroying the harmonious balance between the right and wrong rules/laws; but our conscience of the moral beliefs, however, remains intact.

In fact, this is what happened to Adam Smith's economic system; its moral foundation is still intact, but his ethical foundation collapsed; that is, his perfectly competitive markets that were supposed to mitigate and suppress the egotistic nature of man—the self-correcting mechanism of greed—"never" materialized on the supply side of the free markets; big businesses and monopolies, driven by greed, destroyed the competitive "nature" of the free enterprise system; what remained was pure, unbridled capitalism!

Many prominent economic thinkers recognized the downfall of the classical economic system, including—in particular—Marx, who succeeded in convincing half of the world that the correct solution was complete destruction of capitalism, to be replaced by revolutionary means, and replaced by state dictatorship; of course, now we know that approach was a complete historical failure—you cannot resolve an economic problem by altering man's nature and destroying his conscience at the same time!

It was John M. Keynes who finally, and without attempting to change man as a human being, brought about a revolution in economic thinking that altered the course of not only economics but the ethical foundation of the free world. His approach was to reinstate the harmonious balance between the public and self-interests; he must find a new mitigating force to impose anew the needed limitations of the greed-driven big businesses to ensure the restoration of the foundation of our ethics. This ethical reorientation, he believed, would not destroy the derailed system but will put it back on its tracks. This, he believed, could be done only by the power of the government—the public sector. For the first time, an economist dared to propose the use of government power—the antithesis to the established free enterprise doctrines—a partnership between the private and the public sectors of the economy—that is, a mixed free economic system, whereby, via the powers of taxation, spending, borrowing, subsidies—the use of monetary, fiscal, trade policies and regulatory controls, the government will be able to design and implement the required policy programs, to restore national economic activity to its desired levels of full employment, price stability, etc. This proposition, in effect, puts the government as the captain of the ship; it charts the economic course of the nation; a vastly new and more powerful role for the federal government, which has a potential to control and, with the possibility of errors due to incompetence, throw the economy into greater crisis. Keynes foresaw such risks and advocated that over a given period of time, the deficit incurred to restore full employment must be eliminated when the economy reaches a full-growth capacity, creating surplus budget(s); in this way, the economy at the end of the cycle will be free of debt! This part of his proposition, in recent years, was conveniently omitted, and with the relaxation of consumer borrowing, we ended up with unprecedented amounts of private as well as public debts that could not be paid, causing debt foreclosures, eroding the confidence and the trust in the entire economic system—causing the second-biggest economic crisis in the world (after the Great Depression)—the Debt Recession of 2008!

It is most unfortunate that Lord Keynes did not leave a blueprint telling us how to deal with debt-induced recession; but it never occurred to him that people and institutions will spend—borrowed money—beyond their ability to pay back. Some have even questioned Keynes's wisdom of marrying the public sector with the private sector, if it really contributed to the elimination of the Great Depression; it was, in fact, the demands of WWII that made the difference. What we really ended up with, as a result of his ideas, was increased government power in the affairs of the economic system; it altered its structure, operations, and purpose, turned it into a target-managed economic system, ruled by political will and purpose.

Today's economic activities certainly cannot be explained by going back to the world that Keynes had to deal with; it is something much more profound and complex that occurred in the entire eco-political system, as a whole, which caused and explains its phenomenal evolutionary change. The entire value system that determined and defined what constitutes economic success experienced a revolutionary change; the rules and guidelines that existed before are now ignored or nonexistent. Bigness now is synonymous with success, but bigness itself has its own weight; it becomes so big that no one can touch it—"it is too big to fail," a case of a state within a state—but, ironically, if it fails because of greedy incompetence, it gets bailed out by the collective political will and power vested in it by the people at their own expense. The bigness-success relationship induced and motivated two unfortunate events to occur too fast before their consequences could be understood and predicted.

First, the idea of globalization is based on the proposition that trade benefits both parties—this did not materialize. Certain countries deliberately manipulated the currency exchange rate to alter the terms of trade in their favour. The rich countries lost the comparative advantage to those manipulators—to the developing countries, by sourcing out to them their manufacturing industries; including the transfer of capital, technologies, management know-how, and ensured markets for their goods and services; this all was done in the name of bigness through globalization. All this resulted in the loss of factories/industries, as well as increased consumption of cheap foreign goods; paid for by credit, causing unprecedented accumulation of debts—private and public.

The difference with this debt is that a good deal of it is foreign debt—the foreigners now own, in that amount, our wealth; we are obligated to them for bailing us out of our economic difficulties, a characteristic of a poor country that could not feed its people! The reputation of a rich/wealthy nation is now degraded—reputation and trust have also diminished accordingly. The global economic dynamics has now shifted from Europe and North America to China and India—a tragic situation, indeed.

Second, the unforeseen consequences of the information technology revolution that succeeded in shrinking the globe into a village, where I am involved and am part of everyone's business; leads to the temptation of wanting what everybody else has—the imitation factor, which opened the gates of emigration—the flow of humanity in search of a dream—the better life!

Flow of ideas
" thoughts
" opinions
" dreams
" hopes

Humanity on the move,
Humanity in motion!

These movements weakened the traditional centers of stability and permanency; the political center of power gives away to the big global power—
the global corporation—roaming free and mostly irresponsibly in a sea of
uncharted and unbridled territory. There is perhaps too much of global
economic and demographic action/activity, but too little and ineffective
global political will and binding action to establish a countervailing global
force/power to determine and enforce uniform worldwide rules of conduct and behavior for those unruly global giants of wealth and power. The
disconnect between the economic world power and the political global
will to act is the most urgent task that needs to be addressed and resolved
before it is too late! If the current trend of global economic concentration
of power continues, we will in time end up with very few world oligarchs
(Russian style), who will not only control the world's economic wealth,
but will, by that very power, control its political destiny as well. Then,
there will be no politics—no democracy, no rights, and no freedoms or
justice.

We have to admit to ourselves that current international organizations and
agreements are, at best, a patchwork of disorganized and disunited points of
references; cannot/do not do the necessary job; and the world is too big for a
single country to dominate and solve its problems. Given the above dilemmas,
what can we do to ensure world order, peace, and tranquility? The question is,
what are our options?

    I.   Retreat from world involvement—bring back our corporations;
         impose tariffs on foreign imports, etc.

    II.   Stay the course, the way things are now, and hope for the best!

    III. Assume the leading role in world affairs—rearrange/realign the global
         alliances, now, before they get too powerful to be influenced.

Obviously, the first option is too late, too dangerous, and counterproductive—
if we withdraw from Eastern Asia, we will leave them to develop (with our
know-how and technology) and probably surpass us!

The second option is equally unattractive; it is too uncertain, unstable, and most likely, we will lose the competition with Eastern Asia.

We are left with the third option as the most viable course of action; provided we accept the following conditions/realities:

<u>One</u>: Democracy is not for everyone—it is a responsible system of government and requires tradition, tolerance, and sacrifices, which many are not ready/willing to commit to—they prefer security.

<u>Two</u>: North America alone cannot solve all of the world's problems; it is necessary to reallocate and share this burden of responsibility with others, based on regional realignment and on the principle of accommodation.

<u>Three</u>: The "new" realignments will be based on the "old concept" of regional spheres of influence and accommodations; based not on ideologies but on economic well-being and humanism.

I.   China has already moved in this direction; it has cultivated and enjoys extremely close relations with Pakistan; when US forces leave Afghanistan, it will revert to Taliban control in unity with Pakistan; Iran is already in that sphere; the only question is Syria; if America does not intervene, it will be next; the former Soviet Muslim republics will join this sphere of mutual interest—they hate the Russians. If the Russians join this sphere, we are going back to the Cold War period, which is not what we want. China may not want to have Russia, because it is a potential rival for predominant leader; also, Russia, as an economic and military power, is far behind China and will slide even further.

II. To devise a countervailing sphere, we must include India, Japan, Taiwan, Australia-New Zealand, Indo-China, Indonesia, Philippines—the entire southeast Asia.

III. The third sphere of mutual interests is the entire continent of Africa and all the Middle East countries—preferably Syria included—we do not want the first sphere to access the Mediterranean Sea.

IV.   The fourth sphere is the European continent, including Russia, Ukraine, Georgia, and Turkey; the problem will be the inclusion of Russia, since the Eastern Europeans hate it because of their oppression by the Russians.

V.   The fifth, of course, is the Americas—north and south.

These five regional spheres are determined on the basis of the size of the population—demography and the natural resources availability.

The mode of their mutual governance shall be the establishment of a governing council (to replace the ineffectual security council of the United Nations), consisting of fifteen members—three members from each sphere; decisions by the council shall be made based on majority rule; no sphere or spheres shall have veto power; the chairmanship shall be on a rotating yearly basis; Switzerland shall be its place of operations. Their decisions shall be binding on all equally; and shall be irrevocable and nonappealable!

The council shall deal with the following world matters and issues:

1.   It shall have the sole responsibility to ensure that there exists and will continue to exist mutual respect and good will among the five spheres.

2.   Establish the basic principles of respect and dignity for all humanity by enumerating the rights and freedoms of the individual and declaring the limitations and responsibilities of the states.

3.   Establish measures to protect the environment.

4.   Establish a uniform process for the reduction of all kinds of weapons of mass destruction.

5.   Establish measures to control the growth of the world's population.

6.   Establish rules of assistance in times of crisis.

7. Space exploration shall be a joint venture and the cost/benefits shall be shared equally.

8. Disputes between spheres shall be resolved peacefully.

9. The unprovoked attack by one sphere over another shall be considered as an attack on all; and will require a countermeasure response by the four spheres.

The implementation of these measures—as determined by the World Council—shall be left to the regional governing bodies themselves. This is to emphasize that this proposal is not intended to create a world governing body, and presumes the acceptance of the current national/state realities and their sovereignty rights. The implementations must, of course, be in agreement and harmony with the intent and the terms of the council's decisions.

The selection of the members of the council—the fifteen members—shall be the responsibility of the individual spheres, three members each. However, to ensure some uniformity, preserve diversity and prevent packing the council with political ideologues, I recommend the following: Each sphere shall select one hundred representatives, based on professional merit and mindful of population diversity and geographical disparities. Once the one hundred representatives are chosen, they shall gather together for the purposes of electing the three World Council members from their own ranks. All council members shall possess a four year university degree and shall be between fifty and seventy years of age while in service.

PART IV
MONEY, BANKING, AND CAPITAL

Money: Its Essence and Significance

Money, that mythical and mysterious thing that rules the world; the root of all evil; temptress of men; unfaithful mistress; the cause of jealousy and envy, greed and desire, a reason to lie, cheat and steal, a motive to betray, murder, and fight wars.

We all want it; believe in it; wish for it, pray for it, gamble for it. We all have it—of course in varying amounts—and use it practically every day. It makes us important, secure and respected. It is the means to new opportunities and options; it brings freedom and independence; it buys influence and prestige; it secures luxuries and comfort, but most of all it brings and gives one power. Power to do, power to be, whatever you wish to do and whatever you wish to be!

Money can practically create or destroy anything and everything. It moves, directs, and manipulates resources and people; their skills and efforts alter existing social relations and create new ones. It arranges, directs, and redirects the movement of all the goods and services that we produce, thus determining the mode of our life and the style of our living.

Money, per se, is neutral and on its own cannot do anything, good or evil. But when put in the hands of men—good and evil men—it can do all! Money, therefore, is the means, the conduit, in fact the mechanism that enables men to do it all: in short it is a facilitator for all of our economic actions and transactions.

The mystery of money lies in the nature of its creation and purpose thereof. It is an abstract thing that has a built-in, concentrated purchasing power that is indestructible. It is a universal, acceptable standard that measures wealth, enables exchange of resources and products by determining their worth or price in that standard. Ingeniously, it transfers perishable surpluses into non-perishable, non-destructible, usable, and secure forms of value that can, and are, used for future transactions. It is its future use that makes it a unique invention. It ties the present economic activities with those expected, future economic activities: the connection of now and tomorrow.

Money, in essence, enables credit to exist and credit is the cornerstone of our modern capitalism: the free enterprise system. In fact, it facilitates and brings together scarce and scattered barter "markets" into a uniform, expanded universal free market system by enabling the buyers and sellers to determine the worth price of their products, etc., in a uniform standard, agreeable and acceptable by and to all!

Generally speaking, money is characterized by its economic functions: first, it has the power to allocate resources and direct the flow of goods and services; second, it represents an abstract built-in power of wealth; and third, the power of wealth can, and is, being used to create new forms of production resource, i.e., capital, and brings about improvements in the other resources. More specifically, however, the role of money is to:

1.   Serve as a unit of account, a universal standard of measuring wealth;

2.   Serve as a medium of exchange—it facilitates the flow of resources and goods and services from where they are idle and useless to where they are useful;

3.   Serve as a store of value—that is, money in gold and silver coins has its own intrinsic value—as precious metals. People may prefer to hold their assets/wealth in this form, to protect the value of their wealth during recessions;

4.   Serve as credit facilitator—it is an accepted means of deferred payment; loan/credit agreements are negotiated and signed in terms of money, the universal unit of account.

The origin/beginning of money-coins most likely occurred in one of the more prosperous and progressive village(s), probably somewhere in Mesopotamia 4,500 years ago. Lydia in about 700 BC used electrum as money. The individual that most likely played a significant role in the initial stages of the evolution of money was the blacksmith. The story goes something like this: Human vanity and religious beliefs motivate, inspire, and compel us to gather, make, collect, and hoard valuable things for decorative and ceremonial purposes/occasions. As the economy improved, people got wealthier and bought and collected more of these valuable things—especially made of silver and gold.

The problem of security arose. How to protect their valuables against another human weakness: thievery. It is, I believe, that first blacksmith, by virtue of his trade, who came to their rescue. It is he that built a strong box for his own, his relatives' and close friends' use. They gathered their valuables, put them in a small, labeled box, which in turn was placed in the blacksmith's strongbox. This, of course, was done on the basis of trust. This trust, however, was put into question as the blacksmith expanded his service to others. As the people brought their boxes, put them in, came back, took them out, things began to get confused, suspicions and accusations began back and forth, etc. This forced the blacksmith to enumerate and give receipts of the contents in the small boxes to the people who owned the boxes. This activity, more or less, forced the blacksmith to be more of an accountant than a blacksmith. Those who chose to stay with the strongbox began to charge for their services. To simplify their accounting process/practices, the most astute and perceptive one came up with an ingenious-innovative solution—after the realization that most of these valuables stayed in the boxes unused—why not melt these idle gold and silver valuable things into uniformed pieces, easily recognizable and easily measurable. This was done with the permission of the owners, of course, by drilling different-sized holes in hardwood, containing different multiple amounts of gold/silver. The amounts were measured in weights—one gram; five grams; ten grams; twenty-five grams, fifty grams; one hundred grams, etc.

These flat and round pieces of gold/or silver, decorated with "pictures," became our first, real money—one gram is our one dollar; five grams is our five dollars, etc.

This is how the first coin money was created, and with its creation the world was revolutionized and would never be the same again. Many wise people believe and attribute the significance of money on par with the discovery of fire and the invention of the wheel; perhaps it is so!

Now, our blacksmith-accountant is our goldsmith and his job is now much simpler. People now bring boxes, but in them we find coins of different sizes or denominations. He takes out a sheet of paper and writes on it the contents of the box, but now exactly: 100 - 10 gram pieces; 1,000 - 50 gram pieces, etc. This piece of paper is signed and given to the owner of the box, and a duplicate is kept by the goldsmith and countersigned by the owner. This receipt, or more accurately a note, is the precursor to our flat (paper) money. The note in fact states that the owner of the note has, on deposit and in trust, the stated amount of gold and/or silver coins with the Mr. X Goldsmith, signed and stamped. Stated differently, Mr. X Goldsmith not only states the facts of deposit but states the commitment to pay the stated amount(s) to whomever the note belongs, i.e., the note is in fact Mr. X Goldsmith's pledge of I owe you (i.e., IOU). People began to use the notes as payments, rather than carry large amounts of coins, which were risky and heavy, simply by writing on the back of the note, giving instruction to Mr. X Goldsmith how to dispose of the gold or silver coins represented by the note, by simply transferring the ownership of the said coins. Today we write the equivalent of "pay to the order of," etc.

As we evolved with time, the issuer of the note changed, keeping up with the economic and financial evolutionary development, which in turn the existence of money made possible. Instead of the goldsmith issuing the note, the goldsmith became a lender of money—a bank. It is the bank that issues the note now; and when you put the bank and the note together, it becomes banknote/banknota, etc., or our official money, issued now by the federal government, the Bank of Canada. So the dollar or the five-dollar bill that you hold in your hand represents an IOU by the Bank of Canada. What, though, does the bank owe you? In fact, it owes you or ought to owe you what goldsmith X owed the note owner—his deposited gold or silver coins. But does it?

What actually made the note acceptable as a medium of payment (money) was that it was totally backed by gold or silver metals, having their own intrinsic value (on the market); that is, their dual use/value made them acceptable as money. This security over time was eliminated because the use of gold and silver as metals increased in value and strength and the government and

Central Banks simply could not afford to buy these metals as backup for the dollar on the free market, at market prices. Thus, today the dollar not only is not backed by bullion, but our coins are no longer made of gold or silver, but of cheaper metals. So, the bank does not have gold or silver for you in exchange for your dollars. Instead it has Treasury bills for you—i.e., for every dollar it coins/prints, the Bank of Canada, by law, has to purchase an equivalent amount of T-Bills. This is more for accounting purposes, i.e., to balance the bank statement, assets vs. liabilities, rather than giving you T-Bills directly for your dollars; since you, with your dollars, can buy the same T-Bills at your local bank. Now, as we all know, the T-Bills are an instrument used by the federal government/finance department to borrow money from us, business, institutions, etc., to make up their deficits; that is, a T-Bill is an IOU—a promissory note to pay back your loan with interest. But, as we have seen, money is also an IOU, so it would seem that our dollar is a double IOU! Indeed, a mathematical miracle, a double (IOUs) negative makes indeed a strong positive—our dollar!

Putting aside the T-Bills as a backing to our dollar, what really makes our dollar, our money? Simply the fact that we use/accept it as money, makes it money. As long as you and I accept and use it as money, then it is money. Why then do we accept it as money? Because we have faith and trust in our economy, in our country. In short, we have trust in one other—the dollar that you give me in payment or change, I accept, not because the Bank of Canada says it is a dollar, but because I know that in order for this dollar to exist, somebody, somewhere in Canada has put an honest effort to produce, provide, and/or create a good or service that is worth a dollar on the market. The dollar represents the efforts of our resources.

If we all stop working tomorrow, all factories, businesses, institutions, stores, etc., will close down; nothing will be produced—no goods and services, etc. What happens to the value of the dollar? It goes down, and therefore buys less and less because inflation sets in, and if we continue not working indefinitely, the dollar will eventually reach a point where it is worthless: we lose confidence in it, faith in each other, and it ceases to be money.

For this reason, it is pointless for the government to buy things to use as a backup, wasting people's money. Money is money, because you and I work, produce things of value and know and trust that we shall continue to do so, as long as we can—we all believe in this, and it is this that backs and determines our dollar as our money!

If money is what you and I say it is, and is because of the efforts that you and I put in the production of the goods and services that have value—market value—and our money simply represents and/or reflects this value in terms of an abstract universal standard—our dollar—then why are our efforts not recognized, depicted, and expressed in/on our money?

In fact, most of our efforts are indeed recognized as most of our financial market transactions are done in terms of checks, drafts, and credit cards that are personal/business arrangements with our banks. It is only the so-called flat money, i.e., government-printed banknotes and minted coins, that do not, as yet, recognize these efforts.

However, this will soon be eliminated when replaced by a new money card. We already have entered the cashless society—no more coins in your pockets and bills in your wallet—only one card in your wallet! A card, combining both your credit card(s) and your debit (client) card into one money card that reflects and represents your income, deposited in your checking account, in addition to the amount of credit that you have arranged with your bank. These amounts represent your income deposit, your efforts and your credit, as well as someone else's efforts transferred to you for your use—i.e., available to you for your spending/buying needs, your expenditures.

The nature of this card is unlike the others: for credit and/or client cards that are the property of the bank, the terms, conditions, and design are the bank's business. Conversely, the income (money) card will be your card, with your own personalized ID information and design. First and foremost, the design must reflect you—not the monarch or the prime minister, etc.—your PIN, your thumb print, your photo (renewable every five to seven years), your signature, and any other security and identification that the bank may want, which, however, ought not overshadow the fact that it is your card and thus your money. The bank's logo must be on it as well as some symbol to identify you as Canadian, since your card will be and will constitute part of the Canadian money supply and its currency.

The card itself will remain the worldwide standard adopted size, but it will be redesigned to give it a more prestigious look and feel. The plastic content will be reduced or totally eliminated and replaced with a thin platinum coating on both sides. The card shall be provided by the bank to each of its qualified customers, either at cost or free, but the card shall belong to, and be the property of the customer, and used according to a prearranged contractual agreement between the two parties. The card then becomes invalid when the agreement becomes null and void, i.e., no positive balance in the client's checking account.

If this works, and there is no reason it should not, then we will have simultaneously struck down two historical wrongs. First, because in the past powerful princes, kings, dictators, etc., insisted that they ought to mint or print their countries' currency, and because they did not know how much of it to make, the required balance between the money economy and the real economy was very rarely realized, causing the well-observed cyclical economic fluctuations. With our personalized money, this problem will finally be corrected, so that the money and the real economies will always be in equilibrium—the expenditures will be based on the income earned, and the income earned will reflect the effort and cost of production. Excesses or shortages of money will no longer exist, preventing the occurrence(s) of unnecessary price shifts, which have traditionally caused erratic business cycles.

Second, the past powerful rulers, in usurping money as their own, took credit for all human endeavors and achievements; the common man got none. Now, the credit will go to those that deserve it—the working people; they earn the income, theirs is the money!

Democracy brought them their hard-earned right to take part in the governing process; the money card will give them their rightful recognition and place in our economy. The money card is our financial and economic future—an economy that is built from the bottom up, and not the other way around (i.e., the wrong way). Albeit, the future is uncertain and unpredictable, so that all we can do is create the system, activate the process, and hope for the best.

Now we must go back to our black/goldsmith and trace the birth of the credit card, i.e., the concept of credit. It is not an exaggeration to say that our modern/ capitalist economy is founded on and rests upon the foundation of credit, and credit cannot be arranged without the existence of our financial institutions, principally the banks. We saw how the gold and silver coins were first created in the beginning of our money journey. Further, as the farmer/artisan takes his excess unspent income to the bank for a deposit in gold and silver coins, he is issued a note of deposit, which itself begins to circulate as a means of payment, until eventually it becomes our paper money. The next step in our evolutionary money process is perhaps the most significant, since it required an extraordinary event to occur—a unique and perceptive observation took place and a daring risk to take advantage of it, setting the financial course for all humanity to follow. This discovery/observation was probably made by a keen goldsmith, who noticed that over time and overall, the amount of coins that people deposited in the strong box always exceeded the amount that they withdrew for their spending needs. That is, the box always contained coins that nobody used— they lay there idle! Suppose, mused the goldsmith, I use it—or some of it—or let my trusted friends use it on a sure deal; nobody would be the wiser, nobody would miss it and it will be restored, no harm done. It is here that we crossed that historical line, from seeing deposits as individual deposits belonging to the people, to deposits as a unit or as a whole belonging to (or at least having control over) the goldsmith to use and control. This change in attitude and law paved the way for the creation and extension of credit, as well as our financial institutions.

The goldsmith, after a few rewarding dips in the box to use the idle coins, decided that honesty in the long run is the best policy and so made the depositors an offer which they could not refuse—instead of them paying him to protect their money, he would pay them "interest" if they would agree to let him use their unused coins in his strongbox. In addition, he would withdraw the protection charges as well. An agreement that seemed to be fair to both parties—its survival to this very day is proof. The acceptance of this offer became the basis for the charter of our banks. It is hard to think of any other agreement, except perhaps the Magna Carta, that has done so much good for us all!

Now our goldsmith is indeed a banker—he not only accepts deposits but also extends credit; no more sneaking into the box as the vault is open to all. And henceforth, it is the implementation of the agreement that will occupy our attention and efforts. How can we most efficiently and effectively match the needs of depositors, those that have a surplus of money and savings, with those that have a deficiency of money, the borrowers that need credit to offset their deficiencies? That is, we must find a home for the unspent/idle money where it will do the most good. Banking is a matchmaking business, like a match-made marriage, with one notable difference: if a marriage fails, only the couple will suffer, but if all banks fail, the entire country, most likely, will suffer.

On the depositor's side of the box, things have not changed much since the goldsmith's days, with the exception of the note of deposit. Now the note itself is different, and is in fact issued by the Central Bank (the Bank of Canada) in a form of our currency—in which we are not allowed to do business! The chartered banks issue investment certificates that have nothing to do with the notes. On the other side of the box, the borrower's side, a great deal has changed, which essentially retells the history of modern banking, i.e., the mechanism of borrowing money, or how to move the surplus that nobody uses and stays idle to an active, useful state?

Of course, you had the option of going to the goldsmith/bank and arranging a loan, and taking the money in gold/silver coins; however, this had its drawbacks; namely, large amounts were impossible to carry as well as risky. A clever banker solved this problem with an innovative instrument, like the note, but not exactly—it did the job of the note, but served the borrower by making it easier to allocate effectively the borrowed money. The bank simply transferred the borrowed amount to the borrower's box/account and gave the borrower pieces of bank forms—today, our checks. One could then, in turn, use these forms/checks to instruct the bank how and to whom to release or allocate your "account" money. In this way, the person to whom you have stated to pay (i.e., "to the order of" recipient) would present your check to the bank and would have the stated amount paid or transferred to their account.

Today, most of our market transactions are done using checks; however, the drawback is that a check is good for only one use and no good for small amounts. Moreover, they are not acceptable in the wider markets, need to be cleared, etc. Something new and better was needed to complement the check, so technology, together with banking ingenuity, provided the answer—the credit card.

The advantages of the credit card are that it can be used repeatedly, is easy to carry, is convenient and is useful for small and for large transactions. However, disadvantages include: it can be easily lost or stolen, it has high interest on unpaid balance, it has a maximum spending limit set by the bank, and finally it is the property of the bank. With the present technological advancements in place, it is also possible to bank by phone and online and arrangements can be made to pay your bills automatically through the bank, on a monthly basis. These are some of the tools that are dispensed when credit has been approved.

To qualify for credit is, of course, not as straightforward. Credit is based, and approved, on the basis of trust, but not a blind trust. The bank has to ensure that you are a trustworthy client before it turns over its money to you, money that belongs, in fact, to its depositors and itself also deposited on the basis of trust. For these reasons, the bank not only charges interest for the use of its money, but it also must ensure that the loan will be paid back, so that it must evaluate your ability to repay the loan, as well as the probability that you will repay the loan (i.e., that you will live up to the terms of your loan agreement). To do this, it must evaluate the following characteristics of, and conditions for, the potential borrower:

1. Character—your trustworthiness, reflected in past credit history

2. Capacity—your future earning potential

3. Capital—your venture risk probability and expected gain

4. Collateral—protection you offer if your venture fails

5. Competition—are there shortages or surpluses of loanable funds in the market

6. Climate—the prevailing financial climate about the future of the economy.

Banking is "a business like any other business," or so banks claim! Clearly it is a business, but it is not like any other, since in total, banks are responsible for the supply of our money; money which we all use and cannot do without. In this way, banks supply and provide a vital service and a product quite unlike, say, the shirt-manufacturing business. The health of the banking business affects the health of our entire economy.

Since it is to their advantage to lend as much as possible, many banks overlend, leaving little for the transaction needs of their depositors, leading to and, in effect, causing a run on the banks. People panic, as they cannot get their money, resulting in a loss of confidence in the financial system: banks close, people hang onto their now "dear" money, the economy is cash-starved and slides into a recession. Coupled with the stock market collapse, the economy went beyond a recession into a depression. According to monetarists Milton Friedman and Anna Schwartz, the Great Depression was due in large measure to changes in the money supply; a drop from 26.6 billion in 1929 to 21.9 billion in 1934. It is for this reason, more than any other, that the government was compelled to establish a Central Bank to monitor and keep in check those banks that cross the line. The Bank of Canada presently sets a required reserve limit for all banks to follow, ensuring the depositors that their money will be there for their use when they want it.

Perhaps this is the place to introduce my favorite story about the origin of the term dollar. A long time ago, in a village called Yakimtaller, somewhere in the foothills of the Carpathian Mountains, a prince was said to have mined for silver and minted silver coins, then called *tallers*. The term *taller*, over time and as a result of distortion of the local dialect/language, was modified initially to *dollers* and then further to *dollars*, as used today. The village's name remained Yakimtaller, however, and may indeed be the place of origin of my grandfather, named Yakim (from Jacob of the Old Testament)—who says history is irrelevant!

The Reason for and the Consequences of Credit

The reason for credit is obvious: people, companies, and institutions borrow from others because they do not have enough to cover their current expenses or to undertake ventures, operations, and/or projects that are above and beyond their current financial ability. Credit gives these people, companies, and institutions a different option, one that did not exist before, which is to undertake the venture now by borrowing, rather than saving for it so as to do it sometimes in the future when enough cash has been saved! Simply put, you can do things now by borrowing and indebting yourself, rather than waiting and doing them tomorrow, debt-free.

Which is better and how does this (credit) choice affect the utilization of our current resources and the resources of our future generation(s)? Before we get into the analysis of these questions, perhaps we should stop and say a few things about the economic system that preceded the money market system to give us a sense of where we came from and why we chose credit!

The Barter System

Barter is an exchange of one thing for another of equal value. For barter to occur, there are certain conditions/prerequisites that must be met and satisfied. These are:

1. To barter, you have to have something to barter with; that is, you have to have a surplus—something that you have excess of, or something that you may use but wish to trade for something else that would be of greater use to you.

2. There must be an existence of coincidence of needs and it must be known by both parties.

3. The two parties must agree on the equivalency of value; that is, the price of one in terms of the other—e.g., five pigs equal one calf (5 p=1c and 1c=5p).

4. The exchange, i.e., buying and selling, takes place at the same time; that is, you cannot sell without buying, and vice versa—the equation of exchange is not split and stays intact.

5. As the surpluses are exchanged, they become useful commodities to the new owners and are automatically cancelled out.

This system prevailed in an agricultural economic environment, characterized by small-village life and a life of self-sufficient, small economic units depending on land and beasts of burden as the main resources for their livelihood and survival. For most, the seasons and their benevolence determined their survival at the margin! The seasons determined the rhythm of life, but the animal power determined the speed of work. The rhythm was repetitive and the speed was constant, imposing an unchanging, stagnant economic environment, which in turn led to social interactions and relationships that were repetitive, demanding, and very strict. The harsh economic realities of survival necessitated and imposed extreme discipline on everyone and in all of their actions and interactions. Tradition became the dominant force in their individual and social lives; customs were established and in turn determined the attitudes and behavior of the old and the new generations, which were the same. The old generation passed on its skills, wisdom, and faith to the new, and so on—change could not, and did not, take place—sameness and boredom reigned supreme!

A village made up of small, self-sufficient economic units—the family (all blood relations), each member doing a variety of chores and tasks, on a land scattered and broken into small pieces throughout the country, producing the necessities for survival, and for very few perhaps a little more, locked in isolation from the rest of the world, except neighboring village(s) and some more distant ones. A village with a common code of conduct, beliefs, and behaviors that were strict, unyielding, and unforgiving to anyone that transgressed. Celebrating traditional and religious holidays such as baptisms, marriages, birthdays/name days, patron-saints days, Christmas, Easter, etc., provided the much needed relief and diversion from a life that was short, harsh, unchanging, stifling, and inescapable.

The classical theory, when stripped of the veil of money, reflects the barter economy, which essentially states that output will always be at the maximum since people are motivated by self-interest and survival; they will work to the fullest and produce the most to ensure their survival, as well as better living conditions for their family. In that pursuit, they tried to produce things that they could trade with others for things that they needed more, but could not produce themselves. These trades would take place with others that had created surpluses of their own, for the same reasons. It would be difficult, but exchange would eventually take place, where each surplus would be used as payment, in kind, for the purchased surplus. The surplus supply, in fact, created its own corresponding surplus demand—in short, supply creates its own demand. There cannot be an unsold surplus supply since for exchange to take place under barter, the equivalency condition of value (or price) must be satisfied and met. Moreover, as stated above, after the exchange, the idle surpluses are no longer idle. They are now useful consumer goods enhancing the standard of living of the trading partners. Hence, overall, whatever is produced is consumed, and an overall excess production cannot occur. The same level of production will continue with the same number of workers as before, making unemployment impossible as the economy is always at full employment.

The introduction of money, however, breaks the equation of exchange in two and renders the logic of the classical theory somewhat doubtful, because now when you sell your calf for cash, you have options:

1. You can still buy the five pigs, using the barter option.

2. You may choose to deny your family pork and buy no pigs at all, taking the gold/silver coins home and stashing them.

3. You may buy three pigs and bring home the rest of the money.

Here, for the first time, money allows us to transform all or some of the surpluses into an abstract indestructible form, which we can take home, hide, and not spend, thus breaking the equation of exchange in two. You can now sell, without buying; conversely, you can buy using your own savings, without selling. This, in turn, destroys the equilibrium between total production and consumption. Now, it is possible to sell without buying, leaving someone's surplus unsold. These unsold surpluses will force their producers to cut down on their production, necessitating the use of fewer workers, thus creating unemployment. The validity and logic of the classical theory, though, is greatly restored with the introduction of the savings or investment market; that is, the money that the farmer takes home after not buying the pigs and after selling his calf, will be available for someone else to borrow and buy the pigs for themselves, thereby clearing the market of the unsold surpluses, and so on.

Essentially, the logic of classical thinking is well suited for small, agrarian, self-sufficient economic units characterized by small surpluses, where dual and corresponding needs are easily identifiable, making exchange possible. If the coincidence of needs is not easily met, the idle surpluses will cause reduction in their output, causing less need for the factors of their production where unemployment of the Factor Resources is the result!

In fact, this is what brought the Soviet economy down to its knees. Since the Soviets' internal allocation of resources and goods and services was based on the principles of Barter, and as their economy expanded, the central planning process failed to match in time the overwhelming coincidences of needs, causing the stocking up of idle surpluses to rot, rust, etc., resulting in inefficiency, underemployment of resources and waste of consumer goods—whatever little there was, anyway—stagnation and eventual collapse of the entire economy occurred.

The emergence of credit was simply due to the realization that our own capacity to create great things is largely insufficient; therefore, if I wish to build or create something important, such as the realization of a dream or a goal, a venture or a vision, I need the help of others. More precisely, I need to use the means that they have, but are not presently using, so that by turning over their means for a given period of time, others allow their idle savings to be made active, beneficial, and productive in the realization of my chosen venture. For the use of these funds, I am prepared to pay interest and give you collateral, for your own protection. In this process, I am also doing a service to the health of the national economy, preventing unemployment of resources by changing the status of peoples' savings from idle to active through investment spending.

The method of achieving this transfer of funds is simple. You agree to transfer your cash savings into my account and I sign an agreement to pay the whole amount back to you within a prescribed time frame, on a monthly basis, with agreed-upon interest. This way I am committing my expected future earnings (or part of it) or gain to repay my debt to you, i.e., I am calling forth my future expected means to undertake this venture. I am undertaking risk, since the future is unknowable and uncertain, so that I am placing a great deal of faith in the future and would therefore need and want a steady, stable, and secure future in order for my venture to be successful. It is here, for the first time in human history, where the faith of the present economic condition is tied to, and becomes dependent on, the expected future economic conditions; this connection is determined by credit. Before the establishment of credit, the current economic condition/activity was, to a great extent, projected and determined by the past economic condition and actions. Tradition provided the connecting rod between the past and the present skills, trades, attitudes, conducts, etc., passed on to the new by the old. Credit changed all that. Now the past is not as important as it used to be. The future is now, and it is what is going to be that will drive and determine our current economic decisions. It is the expectation(s) of the future that will determine whether I take on a mortgage to buy a house or take out a loan to build a plant to manufacture shoes, etc.

Our lifestyle and outlook are directed toward tomorrow, because tomorrow, and its expected status, determines our present-day, actual, status. This presents enormous difficulties for us that our forefathers did not have. They simply moved, making the transition from one reality into their new reality, using and relying on their parents' reality as a foundation or stepping-stone. Today, most of us do not have that stepping-stone; we have to create our own foundation and stepping-stone. It is the concept of credit and its process that has become the means to enable us to borrow from others, helping us to create that missing stepping-stone. Today, we stand on our own stepping-stones and shake in fear that it may sink under our own feet, because its strength depends not on our existing, concrete reality, but on a future that is full of uncertainties, speculations, doubts, and hopes, altogether not constituting a very solid foundation to stand on with confidence and certainty. On the contrary, the foundation is based on pure speculation—highly uncertain and highly risky. The risk element is extreme and exacting, perhaps for no other reason than those that risk by borrowing and subsequently succeeding in their endeavors deserve to keep their rewards. They dared to do what no one else dared. Why should they not be able to bask in their glory of success? Yes, certainly they should, not unlike the climber who reached the top of Mount Everest, honestly, courageously, and by his own effort and determination—how you make the journey is as important as getting there!

Since a decision to borrow and invest is for the purpose of serving tomorrow's market, for the needs of the future generation, it is the latter that stand to get the benefits of our present decisions; it therefore stands to reason that if we decided not to borrow or invest, these services and products would not be available to them at all. A great deal of borrowing is also done for the purposes of the current generation, e.g., mortgages. Mortgages help me buy a house and allow me to make (and enjoy) a home now, instead of waiting until I am old and my daughter is grown up! Also, the house is an investment that she will inherit. So, in this way, I am not cheating her out of anything—a home now, an inheritance tomorrow. The problem of the future generation, and even our current generation, arises in the previous factory example: if it is built, everything is fine, but suppose it is not built, then what! Are we cheating the future generation in some way because of this factory deficiency? Many probably would say yes! But is it that simple? Suppose there were no savings to borrow to build the factory, are we still cheating the next generation? Of course not. The same applies to my decision to buy, or not to buy, the house. These are personal and business decisions made by the current generation with respect to the following two points:

1. Savings are necessary for investments. That is, somebody has to make a decision to sacrifice his or her current consumption spending and/or satisfaction in order to put something aside and save;

2. Somebody else has to decide to undertake the risk to borrow someone's savings (indebting themselves) and spend it on a venture that is, at best, uncertain. Whatever we decide to do is certainly our right; the future generation may not like it, and so be it! However, as human beings and good parents, we ought to strive to leave the world a better and wealthier place for our children than the one that we inherited from our parents.

Having said this, however, the real concern by some about cheating or burdening our children lies in another area, that of the government's borrowing and/or living off credit, the deficits that it creates and their consequence(s) on our children, the future generation. The real question is this: Is government borrowing the same as that of the individual, the business companies, or not? Does the government's budget logic rest on the same principles as the logic that determines and defines the budgetary constraints of the family, of the business? The answer is most probably, no, because family and business spending (including borrowing) is limited by their earning/revenue limits on a yearly basis. The government, on the contrary, has no such limitations. It can get more revenues via an increase in taxes and/or by borrowing money from people, businesses, institutions, and foreign financial markets. Its revenue constraint is very elastic. The method of government borrowing is very much like my mortgage agreement with the bank. I signed a commitment to pay back the principle borrowed sum plus interest—a commitment for the future. The government (in effect its Treasury Department) sells you a T-Bill, or a promissory note, that it will pay you back the amount stated on the T-Bill plus the interest shown after a given maturity period. The government takes your cash and you walk away with the piece of paper. Congratulations, you have contributed to the national debt. What have you done? Have you placed a burden on your children? This is the question.

When the government goes into debt to cover its expenses, it goes to the financial money market where you and businesses borrow. To borrow the money it needs, the government sells IOUs or T-Bills. Thus, the government competes with you for the same funds; most likely, the government will outcompete you because it can offer better terms. The result here is that we have a reallocation of funds—resources from the private sector to the public sector—fewer tractors and more tanks, so to speak. The cost of borrowing will most likely be higher with the government as a competitor than without, for the same funds. Now, obviously, the children will inherit fewer tractors, and their ability to produce more potatoes will be somewhat curtailed. However, they will inherit more tanks and will be given greater security. This becomes, in effect, a value judgment that we have to make: do we want more government services or do we want more private consumer/capital goods and services?; which are more important to us, now, and for our children, tomorrow? Certainly, there are good arguments for and against either side.

In a democracy, we have agreed that the best way to resolve this dilemma is to entrust the power to make these decisions in our elected representatives. It is their responsibility to seek and achieve the required balance between the public needs and private wants. Public debt, if carried to the extreme, may threaten this delicate balance. We can easily slide from a free enterprise system to a government-dominated and government-directed economy. The dangers of creeping central control into not only our economic life but also into political and social control and the dependency-on-government factor are very serious and must be stopped. The government, via deficits, is robbing the private sector and denying it to reach and achieve its full potential. For these reasons, the government must be limited in its scope and activity with respect to the rest of our personal, family, and business activities. I have argued in another essay/article how this can be achieved. Simply stated, we must define the tasks and responsibilities of the government precisely and limit them to a few, such as security, health, and education, and arrange a better and more meaningful relationship between labor and business, where their partnership will take care of their health needs and the educational needs of their children.

The question of balance between public and private needs and wants is of great concern to us, as well as to the future generations. The issue that we are trying to clarify, however, is how, or whether, we the current generation somehow hurt, cheat, or burden future generations through yearly deficits, the national debt. Putting aside this concern, some claim the manner in which we pass the burden to our children is through the interest on the public debt, which the latter have to continue paying in addition to the principal amount until it is fully paid off at maturation date. Why should they be saddled with such a burden when it was we that created these debts for our own use and purposes? The question is fair, and the answer is also fair and simple. We not only leave them a burden but also assets, in approximately equal amounts—the interest that the government will pay to discharge our borrowing obligations will be paid to those children that inherited T-Bills from their parents. The problem as a whole that the future generation faces is one of income redistribution, and possibly a goods and services shift, in favor of the public sector as opposed to the private sector. If we assume that the people who pay the taxes to pay the interest on the public debt are the same people who inherit the T-Bills and consequently receive the same amount in interest as they paid in taxes, then we have a cancellation of the burden by the equal amounts of the benefit.

However, the probability of this happening is quite low. In reality, it is the wealthy parents that buy the bulk of the T-Bills and leave them to their children, who collect the interest paid by all the children. It is not fair to those children that will pay taxes for the government to pay off the interest on the previously accumulated national debt and receive no interest because their parents were too poor to invest in T-Bills. At first glance, this argument sounds good; however, the following points show what is wrong with it:

1.   The government most likely went into debt because it did not wish to cut certain government programs, or wished to increase government programs for, especially, low-level income groups. The poor child who is paying taxes continues to benefit from these programs, which without these deficits would have been cut off.

2.   On the progressive income tax scale, exemptions, and deductions, the poor child's tax is not that big.

3.   Assuming there was no deficit, the amount borrowed by government from the rich would have most likely been invested in another business enterprise, leaving their children an inheritance possibly larger than the T-Bill inheritance, with fewer government services, of course.

4.   The parents that purchased the government T-Bills invested in the public sector, thereby denying themselves the use of these monies for other purposes. They are then being rewarded for that sacrifice, and that reward passed on to their children, which is fair, is it not?

Of course, the real problem is the great disparity in wealth as well as income between the rich and the poor. The deficits may affect that great divide, but the effect is but a slight one. In fact, if the rich do not buy T-Bills, spending in the public services will be that much less.

It is difficult to see how we can unload our burden on our children since it is impossible for us to call forth their as yet undeveloped and unrealized skills, abilities, and resources for us to use and exploit. What we enjoy and have today we produce and create today, with our own real efforts, skills, and resources.

Ultimately, to avoid some of the difficulties/concerns stated above, the government should borrow only for specific and urgent national needs. It can also borrow, however, with great care to improve the efficiency and the workability of the government's fiscal policy, especially when the economy is experiencing recession/depression conditions. Once the economy is healthy, the government ought to right away pay back the debt. We must guard against the falsehood of the sugar daddy syndrome that through deficits, we can all live wealthy and healthy lives. The fact is that we have a given amount of resources and with these resources we can produce only so much during a given timeline, and that is all. Our concern is to make the best and full use of those resources in that period.

Recently, and at the end of thirty to forty years of deficit and accumulation of enormous national debt, surpluses are beginning to show; however, it seems that we have become so used to deficit conditions that this welcome news of a surplus threw us into a tailspin and we are uncertain what to do with the extra money: pay down the debt, reduce taxes, and/or spend it on more/new government programs?

The second concern seems to be of a more serious nature, namely, as the yearly deficits turn into national debt, we have created a bond market; that is, buying and selling these debt certificates to each other, an investment money market for those of us that are more cautious investors, to make a dollar or two. If we pay off the national debt, we are in effect closing down the bond market. This creates two questions: the first, what are we to do?; the second, what happens to the government's monetary policy if there is no bond market?

Both of these questions are valid and important questions, but they are not critical, because monetary policy and its effectiveness do not rely solely on the security market; they also rely on the setting and altering of the reserve requirement that ensures sufficient spending money for the depositors and establishing and altering the bank's rate at which it lends money to the chartered banks. Through the use of moral suasion and shifting the government accounts to and from the Bank of Canada and the chartered banks, the supply of money is altered, thereby affecting the cost of borrowing (the interest rate), which in turn induces us to spend more, or less, on investments and consumption, resulting in the swaying of the national economy in the desired direction!

Of course, the loss of the bond market as an option for a more secure and steady investment will be missed, but this can be easily replaced through the banks, trusts, etc., issuing more and more widely spread guaranteed income certificates (GICs). In effect, if these certificates are done properly, this could lead to the creation of an income certificates market, replacing the bond market altogether, and possibly forever. However, this eagerness to write off the national debt is highly premature, and most likely will not happen because it is a well-loved mechanism by politicians, as they use it to get elected. In particular, they promise many things with respect to the national debt to the electorate, but once elected, they refuse to raise taxes to pay for those promised things, and resort to the easiest way out—to borrow the money. And if the promise to pay off the debt were to occur, it would take time—I refer to President Clinton's surplus projections that were of course wiped out by President Bush in no time at all, with the deficit returned.

At any rate, it is irresponsible to argue that the government incurs deficits in order to not adversely affect its monetary policy: national debt for the sake of monetary policy!

The Nature and Signi.ficance of Capital

It is the culmination, the bringing together into a unified whole, that made possible the capitalist market system: the existence of money, the evolution/creation of markets and the creation of credit through the banking process. The money broke down the constraints of barter, the markets made possible trade by determining the prices of the marketable products, resources, and services, and credit made possible the full use of resources, the allocation of unused/idle money to be put into valuable investments—the creation of capital, a factor of production that did not exist before!

The nature of capital is its embodiment of the sacrifice required in its production—a process of connecting the present with the future. That is, a commitment of the expected future returns to create a productive factor now, and to use it now, for a better tomorrow.

The prerequisites of this process are:

a) There must be dissatisfaction with the current way of life/existence—only dissatisfied people are moved to new and daring challenges and action(s).

b) The creation of a surplus/savings—a sacrifice of the current standard of living and/or leisure time; that is, reallocation of effort, resources, and time, and their reapplication(s).

c) Foresight, inventiveness and entrepreneurial visions, ideas, and abilities to envision the usefulness/purpose of the new means of production.

d) The necessary courage and daring required to undertake the risky venture to its final "profitable" end.

A simple story will illustrate the validity of these prerequisites. Let us go back to the tribal way of (survival) life, settled in earthen dugouts by the river, fishing for a living, where the daily routine is split into eight hours of fishing, eight hours of sleep and eight hours for leisure activities. Traditional values prevail: the men fish, the women do housework. Assume they have tools, spears, knives, and axes. Now, observe two neighbor families, also friends—A and B. Family A enjoys life, is satisfied, finds beauty in nature, the river, the flowers, the birds, etc. Family B is dissatisfied, unhappy with life, nature is threatening, intimidating, and dangerous; they are restless and uneasy, the man finds his leisure time of eight hours wasted time. After much contemplation, thinking, and planning, he decides to make a sacrifice, reduce his leisure time in half and add this saved four hours to a more useful function, fishing. Working on the assumption that the previous catch from eight hours of fishing was enough to feed the family, the extra four hour catch is a surplus of fish, and in order to protect it, the man B cordons off a pond by the river and keeps the extra fish there. In six months' time, the man B has collected enough surplus fish to feed the family for two months without needing to fish at all. The essential question here is, what does family/man B do with the new free time, does he squander it on frivolous activities, or does he envision an idea, an enterprise, discovery, etc., and put it into action. Our family man B certainly is not a squanderer. He is restless and eager to put his idea/project in action. He takes his rudimentary ax and goes to the nearby forest, chooses the biggest tree and starts to cut it down. It takes a long time but finally the tree is cut down. He measures four of five paces and trims it. He then starts chiseling out the insides and eventually digs out a canoe. With the help of his friends, he drags the canoe in the river by the village. Meanwhile, his wife has made a net from vines.

In the river by the village, there is something that is man-made and did not exist before and it will revolutionize the village, its way of life, relationships, and interactions between all the members of the tribe and their standard of living. How did all of this come about; how was the boat built? Simply through family/man B's process—dissatisfaction, vision for change, perception, logs float on the river, need for extra fish, surplus creation used as a means to the realization of the vision/invention!

Now for the first time we see a man with a net, deep in the river, catching fish, and plenty of fish. What to do with this sizable surplus of fish? Simply, he makes an offer to the other members of the tribe that they cannot refuse. To some he offers twice as many fish as they catch in their eight hours of fishing if they agree to work for him to help him build a two-story hut for his family, to others, he gives a similar offer to dig a ditch from the river to bring water by his house, so that his wife will no longer lug water from the river to the house. To the wise old medicine man, he gives all the fish he needs if the latter will teach his children the wisdoms of the ancients, with a promise from him to build a special hut for all the children to be able to go and learn from the wise old man. To his neighbor-friend he makes a special offer to come fish with him in his boat and in return, he will get three times his eight-hour catch. After some reluctance and hesitation, the neighbor agrees. The catch, with his neighbor at his side in the boat, again multiplies. With this new, extra surplus, he gets others to go to the forest, cut down the biggest trees and carve out new canoes and hires others to operate them. This time the catch increases exponentially and the village is saturated with fish—what to do? The answer: of course, use the boats as transportation to take the surplus up/down the river to other tribes and sell it there—opening up new markets.

In due time, their journey brought them face-to-face with other like-minded entrepreneurs—meat, wheat, etc., trade flourished among these peoples, so that their standard of living increased, changing forever their old lifestyle. In fact it eventually disappeared. Their life got better, but for each, not equally. The family/man B now is much different than the rest of the tribal members. He is rich, powerful, respected, and most likely is now the chief of the tribe, since in one way or another, they all work for him; he is the boss and they are the workers. Herein lies the secret, the key, of capitalism; it enables one man to rise among equals, supremely above all of them, and in effect, boss them, direct them, control them, and tell them what to do, how to do it, and when to do it. For the first time, man puts another man under him and becomes his lord, without the use of force, but mere economic advantage. Why and how this revolution happened is clear from the above analysis, but essentially it is the creation, the ownership, and the appearance of the boat in the middle of the river, i.e., the capital, that did not exist before.

It did not take long for dissatisfaction to surface and arguments to begin. Now, the standard for measuring worth is no longer in terms of power, but has become that of wealth, and wealth is easy to see, recognize, and envy. Divisions are established, argued, justified, countered, fought over, and consolidated, but in the end they stay, harden, and never are resolved. Those that sided with the rich—capitalist—argue that he deserves what he gets/has because he had the idea, made the sacrifice, and created the boat, risking his surplus, and used it wisely. Furthermore, he treated everybody well and fairly in making him or her an attractive offer, which they accepted without coercion, yielding a much improved standard of living. Any bad feeling is simply jealousy and nothing else. Ultimately, those that complain are not right and do not have a case for grievance. Those that sided with the rich family/man B, over time became known, and were labeled as the capitalists and/or the free enterprisers, the conservatives, the people on the right. Those who took the other side, the dissatisfied side, argued that we work hard and without them he would be nowhere. It is their labor and skill in manipulating the boat that is important, not the boat itself—an empty boat in the river is merely an empty boat in the river. Moreover, the division of the catch is not fair, as most of it should go their way. Those that argued this side took refuge in the socialist left. Marx provided the ideological treatise in his Communist Manifesto (which in the end did not serve their cause much). It is actually within this controversy that the relationship between men and natural resources is spawned, created as a result of the introduction of the entirely new factor of production, man-made vs. nature-made. This fact, at the outset, placed capital at odds with the nature-made resources, which in the minds of the people are more important, superior, have divine sanctity, and are an end in their own right.

Capital certainly cannot be compared to such natural entities, since it has no such traits. Certainly, there is no comparison between the two in their creation. There is, however, an obvious comparison in their use/utility. The role of capital as a tool is to keep man becoming more productive, reduce his natural time, human and social constraints, so that he can become a more perfect human being. When used in this way, there is no dispute between the capitalist and labor views; however, typically and in many respects and instances, it was not. The problem began from the very first time capital was introduced and how it was applied, especially when it was integrated with the other tribespeople, or labor. The offer made by family/man B to the others, particularly to his neighbor-friend, was perhaps fair and tempting; however, it should not have been accepted in the exact way it was presented, i.e., it is the acceptance of a wrong proposal for the wrong reason(s), or short gain, which led to the still irresolvable conflict between labor and capital. This agreement split the interests of labor and capital forever, and made them bitter enemies when, ironically, they need one another: a boat without man navigating it is useless, but a man on a log in the water is not only sometimes useless, it is risky. This divisive conflict freed both parties to feel no responsibility for one another. The capitalist paid the worker in money (in our story, the fish) and leaves it at that. This confused the rhythm and way of life in the village. But will this new capitalist need this worker more, and on what basis will his old way of existence remain an option, or will it be swept aside by the new way—what, in effect, is the new way? If these people had posed these questions at that time, the agreement that they signed on would most certainly have been different. All that was needed for Family/man B was to offer, say, a 10 percent share in the boat rather than triple a typical eight-hour catch, with the corresponding commitment, risk-bearing agreement, maintenance, and marketing arrangements on the part of the neighbor-friend. In this way, the two would be tied in partnership, not only in capital ownership, but in labor as well.

Perhaps, had the village people known the outcome of their venture, they may have done it the right way, but the fact is that it was not done correctly and more surprisingly, somehow through the ensuing centuries, we failed to correct this historical wrong. Perhaps, once again, it is not too late for us. Our destiny is to go forward in civilization, and by the grace of God, we have to journey together; however, if we leave some behind, they will slow us all and they will determine the pace of our progress. We must provide for everyone the opportunity to undertake that journey with us, by ensuring their security, health, and education, by securing our natural freedoms, thereby our humanness. Greater equality in sharing the common wealth must occur; the extremes between the rich and the poor is an embarrassment and a disgrace for our pretensions to civilization and humanity. Private wealth and control of unfathomable amounts and proportions is not explainable and, further, cannot be explained or justified, under any circumstance. No individual, idea, innovation, concept or design could be worth billions of dollars, as what we know or can do is the result of our collective efforts and creation; no man is worth tens, hundreds of millions of dollars per year, no matter what he may do, think, or feel. For these reasons, maximum limits must be set. It is a myth that those that are paid the top salaries, with the additional inclusion of perks and stock options, are the most capable, creative, and productive people and therefore deserve these granted rewards. They receive these extreme benefits because they control the corporation's board of directors. In fact, it is the board of directors and the stockholders to whom, in theory at least, they are accountable, who themselves are too diverse, dispersed, and disorganized for such accountability to be effective. One simple but effective way of reining in the CEOs' greed is to take away their board's right to determine their own salaries, by instead giving the stockholders the right to constitute a separate and independent remuneration committee, separate from the board of directors, and responsible solely to the stockholders directly. This committee would set and determine the annual compensation for their CEO and such compensation would include, among other factors, the company's success.

Conversely, it is imperative to assert that the whiners must stop whining and start doing and acting like responsible, skillful, and competent individuals. They cannot continue forever to hide behind the veil of unfairness and exploitation theories, and should stop being martyrs in order to gain pity. They cannot expect benefits from someone else's efforts, risks and darings. They simply must rise to the challenges of their destinies and respond resolutely with passion and purpose.

This story gives a glimpse as to the origin and the beginning of capital, in addition to the emergence of the continual and unending conflict between labor and capital and the arguments to justify the rightness of each side. However, to illustrate more precisely and effectively the roles that capital, the markets, and money played in the creation of urban life, or the urbanization movement, we must fast-forward to a period closer to our own, i.e., a time that has markets and real money, not fish. This is, then, the story of the farmer's son—bright, intelligent, an active and daring young man, full of ideas, energy and perceptions, but most importantly is very bored and unhappy with farming and farm life. He wishes to create something new, in particular a new way of living. He is familiar and very knowledgeable in farm (peasant) life and living; in the village there is a market where people like his father take their extra stocks, grains, hay, and fruit for sale or trade; coins are used for and as a medium of payment. The biggest nonland business is the mill, and the miller is an important and respected member of the community, but the mill business is a family (not community) concern and is by the river, away from the centre of the village.

Our young man has an idea that is similar to the miller's, but is also in many respects different. He sees that at his father's home/farm there are many different chores and tasks to be performed, some interesting, some very hard and some simply unpleasant and dirty—those that nobody wants to do but will not go away! Perhaps he might be able to do something about it. He has an idea, but requires his father's, and the community's, cooperation. He knows that in the village, people like to eat meat but nobody likes to kill, skin, and cut up the animals that provide them with meat. But these are their animals. His idea, then, is to relieve them of this very unpleasant task by building a slaughterhouse; he would buy their animals, slaughter them, cut them up, and package/wrap at least some and sell the finished product on the market in his village, and possibly in the neighboring villages. But the problem is that he does not have money for such an undertaking; he knows his father would help, but his savings are not enough. He also knows that the other families in the village also have savings, hidden somewhere in their house (there are no banks as yet), because like his father, most of them have taken their surpluses to the market and sold them for money—silver/gold coins. They would have used most of their coins to buy the things they lacked at home, but saved what was left to take home and hide it. (At this time, money has freed the farmers/peasants from the barter constraint, i.e., buying and selling at the same time. Now those with money and goods can buy and not sell, sell and not buy, etc.) The young man decides that somehow he has to get the coins that the farmers/peasants were hiding and make use of them to buy the needed land, lumber, and to hire people to build the structure, also to buy the animals and hire workers to do the unpleasant job of preparing the final product for the market. However, people did not want to readily risk and entrust their hard-earned savings, which they kept for unforeseen events.

They wanted some tangible collateral. Thankfully, his father came to the rescue and put up some of his land for the needed collateral. With commitments made and money collected, our young man is on his way to becoming a business-man, running a business enterprise, and a capitalist, and most importantly is now on his way to building a town, and later a city. How did all this happen? Not easily and a long, long time coming! It is our young man, and many like him, that dared to dream of a different world and better life that envisioned a new way of doing and producing things, and providing services to the people around them, escaping the confines of tradition, the land, and the beasts of burden. These people not only had the idea/the vision but also saw where the means of implementation lay. It was collected, having been scattered and idle in many households, into one (huge) bag of coins used then to create some-thing new like a factory, a means of production concentrating dispersed tasks throughout the village in one single place and all under one roof, producing a service/product needed by the community. The method of production here is now different from that on the farm, i.e., the multitasking of each member of the family, based on the idea of division of labor, into single-task workers, and the resulting breakup of the whole process of production, into more manage-able phases. In short, specialization of labor, supported by technical/mechani-cal tools. The rhythm of production now changes from the rhythm of the beast of burden to the precise rhythm of technology and machines, not an easy tran-sition to make!

The farmer's son and many like him did not spring out of nowhere; it was a long and slow process, but it prevailed out of tenacity and the belief that their new way is the right way—the efficient and more productive way, as compared to the old, slow, hard and boring way. It was not easy to pioneer something inno-vative and threatening, but they overcame all the obstacles. They bought the land, built the factories, designed the layouts, bought and slaughtered the ani-mals, hired the workers (those dissatisfied with farm work), paid them wages, packaged the meat, took it to the market, sold it, received revenue from sales, paid back their loans, and eventually paid wages and paid for the animals and for other expenses. Whatever was left, if anything, was the return for their idea, risk, and efforts—the (so-called) profits.

The creation and the existence of a single factory did not lead to the develop-ment of urban life, but it was the basic and central agent for that development.

This catalyst agent had to be supplemented by two other important events for urbanization to occur:

1. The people that were hired to work in the factory were dissatisfied and in search of a new life, a different life. What they did, how, and for what was diametrically different from what they did on the farm/land. They felt, and became different, which is why they could not work in the factory, or in their new reality, while continuing to live on the farm, and exist like farmers/peasants; the two realities had to go their separate ways! They were now wage earners working under contract for fixed hours, doing the same thing most of the time and excelling at it; they had no worries after work, and that free time was now theirs. But what to do to get off the farm and out of father's house? The new employer resolved the problem, as he made available some of his land (and/or bought extra) for his employees, and with, perhaps, some financial assistance to build shacks/cottages as their new residences, conveniently in the proximity of his factory, the place of their employment.

2. The second event, as important, was the emergence of other, many other, new factories, doing and performing other "needed" products and services that the farmers could not or did not want to do, but they could and did better, much better. The sum aggregate of all of these factory activities and the settlements around them, including married couples and children, required new and different services from the community; they needed schools, churches, banks, trades people, stores, and transportation facilities (roads, sidewalks), in addition to teachers, priests, and health facilities (doctors, nurses, and hospitals), and so on. In time, this new community would need and have its own governing structure and process.

This new community is not, in any way, shape or form, like the peasants' village. It is in fact an urban dwelling place, a lifestyle that we know today as city life. Its basic source of existence is the factory—capital—and not the land. The two means of production are related and dependent on one another; they are in fact married to each other by trade, but are different in essence, origin, and purpose. Peasant/farm life is based and dependent on the land and its generosity (or lack thereof), the latter worked by the economic unit of the highly self-sufficient family, which lives mostly on or at the margin of existence. The work done on the farm is itself founded on the jack-of-all-trades, but master of none, basis. Here, motivation is survival and hope of inheritance as everything, including man, is nature's cause and effect. This is not at all the case with the new Urban setting: life here is determined and dependent on the factory, or capital, and its efficient application to production, based itself on the principles of division of labor, specialization of both labor and mechanisms. Here, motivation is gain through useful work and better living conditions and standards; payment is in terms of money and hired labor does work on a contractual basis, where the labor market determines wages. Man in conjunction with the free market is the cause and its effect.

The success of the new urban reality depended not only on its own performance but on the performance of the rural sector as well: the progress of the two was unwittingly dependent on the simultaneous progress of each. For the factory to get workers for its own use, the rural economy had to free those workers from the farm/land, through increasing the productivity of those that remained on the land to ensure enough food production for themselves, as well as for those now living in the urban towns. The urbanization movement essentially refers only to those forces (economic and social) that provided the foundation and the process to establish the urban lifestyle and should also include the additional changes in the economic and social forces of the rural life that supported that movement. Without the corresponding increase of output in the agricultural/rural sector to free the needed labor for the factories, so as to not have to stay on the land to produce food for them, those factories would not have been built. These interdependence became much stronger and as urbanization became much more sophisticated and mechanized, the cities built farm machinery especially for use by farmers, which in turn increased their productivity, yet again freeing more and more people to migrate to the cities knowing that there would be enough food to live on.

In fact, today many farms are equipped and managed by private business enterprises, and some entirely on a corporate basis; the fundamental basic principles that underlie and define farming and other businesses are very much the same. Here we have a case and a situation where the core nature-created factor of production, land, has successfully combined with the new man-made factor of production, to ensure not only the survival but also the progress of both.

Labor, also a natural factor of production, failed, though, to come to terms with capital and consequently failed to reach a peaceful resolution of their respective positions—each claims preeminent position and importance in the role and contribution they make to the production of the country's wealth and so both make their (justified) claim for their share of that wealth. As we progress with time, their combined efforts, creativity, and drive resulted in an ever-increasing ability to produce more through factories, banks sprung up and facilitated more and easier credit, trade expanded to, initially, the immediate villages, then expanded further afield till it was globalized, as today. This in turn necessitated the creation of transportation and communication facilities, animal power and speed having been long ago outpaced, outpowered, and outdistanced by our mechanical and technical inventions. Farmers synchronized and adopted the use of their land for growing everything for their self-sufficiency to a single best-use basis. It is capital more than anything or anybody that is responsible for the globalization of trade and the great degree of international interactions/interrelations, because it is based on the division of the productive process into smaller and more manageable/mechanized units of performance—the specialization of not only the production of goods and services, but the use and application of all the resources and factors of production. It is that, which caused the creation and production of wealth in unprecedented and unimagined amounts and diversity.

The downturn to this is, however, the total destruction of the traditional world order and its social, moral, and individual values. Our dependency, security, and belonging to the farm/land are gone! We now depend on others that we do not know or have never met for our survival, to produce goods for us and to buy ours in turn. A great insecurity has overcome us, and is overwhelming us all! A great global inter-reliance and interdependence weighs very heavy on all of humanity. Global helplessness is the result of this process. For a secure world, predictable order is required, but is not present and is not likely to be as long as the politicians and their misbegotten, misguided ideologies continue to pit labor against capital and vice versa, and as long as labor leaders blindly follow leftists' beliefs. The time is long overdue for the two disjointed partners to become true partners, to care, share, and protect their common interest and common industry, for it is they that are responsible for trade, transportation, and communication, which in turn leads to the dissemination and dispensation of knowledge, beliefs, experimentation, and discovery—the fundamental ingredients that created our civilizations. Banded together, men began on the road to civilization unknowingly and unintentionally in order to ensure their survival through security. It was within this togetherness they discovered that by dividing their daily tasks, they could indeed do much more, collectively and for all— the breakthrough of specialization. Thus, civilization is built on the principle of the division of labor, which results in a surplus of output, freeing men to seek, create, and become civilized.

The reasons and hence the barriers that caused labor's and capital's failures to come together and be in agreement with one another are numerous and too deep for us to analyze in entirety and resolve here. It is ironic, however, that any two factors meant to live in harmony and complete unity and are created for each other end up being nothing without each other. Capital, in any shape or form, is a tool; it is a place or a gadget that labor uses and drives to perform a task or a function, itself part of an entire process meant to build a (better) product or create a (more efficient) service. Labor and capital work together for that purpose. The problem lies in their ownership; they do not belong to one and the same entity. Labor belongs to the individual and it is the individual that does not wish to recognize or accept that his person and his skills are effectively two separate and distinct realities and that the employer is interested only in one and is willing to pay for only that one, and not both. Conversely, the two are located in one living body and where one goes the other goes also—they are inseparable and their separate needs and abilities are joint. The market, however, treats them separately and establishes the value of only one, the skills that the person possesses, and what these skills will contribute or add to the productive process, how much the market will say it its worth. It is this added value to the output that in turn determines the wage level of the worker's skills. Only the skills are rewarded because they are useful to the employer, not the entire being, although it is man that carries, owns, develops and applies these skills. Therein lies the irresolvable dilemma of labor. Capital does not have this dilemma; its ownership and application are separate entities. They are not vested in one living body, the capitalist or the individual that owns the capital, i.e., the factory. But the factory is not part of his body, which has its own separate needs and function. He is not only separate from his tool (the factory), but, legally, he has, or more correctly, society has created a separate legal entity—a company—to assume the ownership and control of that tool/factory. Capital, thus, is totally, humanly, and legally separate from the person. Therein lies the strength of the capitalist. Labor, though, has not been able to achieve such divestiture and incorporative status. Perhaps some of the professionals have come a step closer to such recognition, but the common worker is not even a candidate for such status.

Now is probably the best time, and high time, for working people to be recognized and given the legal status that would separate their person from their skill/trade/profession, since it is that which they offer as a productive/creative tool on the market; it is that for which they are paid. The idea is to incorporate the skills/trades/professions as legal entities, or as agencies, enterprises, and partnerships, in exactly the same way and manner as the business enterprises have done it for such a long time as legal corporate entities. For example, I am a professor and teaching is my job. I got hired and am paid and it ends there. But I have invested time, money, and effort in acquiring my education, skills, and my capital. Why cannot I register, and thereby have society recognize, this capital as a separate entity from me the person, and then have my college hire my agency that owns and controls these skills, by signing a contract with it.

The advantages to me and my family would be considerable; not only will I be able to deduct expenses for tax purposes, avoiding double or triple taxation, and buy my car, house in my incorporated name, giving me protection in case I lose my job and cannot meet my mortgage payments—a corporate bankruptcy protection, if you will, and a chance to save my house! But perhaps, most importantly, I, as a person, an individual, am legally and otherwise separated from my earning (living) skills, which in today's thinking and terms determine who I am, what I am, and where I am on the social ladder; stigmatization, characterization, and compartmentalization will be greatly reduced by such legal incorporation.

With this and my earlier proposals addressing greater and better lifelong educational and health-care opportunities, the common person will be viewed in an entirely different light and will regain his or her individual character, self-respect, confidence, worth, and dignity as a human being.

As a final point, capital did not play the game of the competitive free market fairly. The market system, through competition, was supposed to self-regulate excessive rewards in the long run through their elimination, thus putting a ceiling on profits. In order for business to escape this market "decency" self-regulation through competition; it, however, resulted in eliminating the competition itself, by creating new market structures that were far less competitive than the free enterprise system suggests, such as monopolistic competition, oligopolies, and regional/national monopolies, via mergers, licensing, patents, resource sole ownership, and regulations, etc. Labor, on the other hand, never could escape the consequence(s) of the undisciplined mentality of the ever-greater multitudes, even through unionization. The law of their diminishing productivity could not be annulled even by Marx's dialectical materialism.

Today, with the collapse of the Soviet Union, even the most die-hard comrades must accept that the annulment of the law of diminishing returns is possible through the creation and the application of capital—the worker is not productive if he does not have the tools. It is that simple. Capital and labor need each other and must resolve their differences together. They must ensure their health (healthy people are healthy workers), their education (educated people are competent workers), and their security when jobless or retired. The companies that were built by their workers cannot endure if they discard these workers after use, without any future commitment. These workers were instrumental in the success of the company and deserve a fair share of that success, such as company stocks, generous severance pay, and/or contribution to their retirement fund/pension.

Finally, labor must accept the fact that capital is the most important factor in the production of our wealth; technology, science, information/communication and transportation facilities, and services are funded and driven by it, and private ownership is the motivation behind it all. The collapse of the Soviet Union proved, conclusively, that government ownership and control is a complete failure and utter waste. Communism failed because of its deceptiveness. It cleverly subverted the real issue—the inner conflict of man, his freedom versus his need for others—and turned it into a social class struggle, the rich versus the poor, the capitalists versus the workers, etc. The resolution of which presupposes the existence of a society that has already managed to resolve the inner conflict of man's nature, and that done then addresses the question of how to best divide the wealth and resolve its ownership question, i.e., the issues of equality and justice. We must first resolve the conflict between man's freedoms and man's rights, achieve the desired/required balance and harmony between the two and then, only then, can we address society's social structure and its performance, the social classes and their interrelatedness. Communism, in its zeal to prove the evilness of capitalism, exaggerated the political importance of capital and conversely undermined its economic significance—that is, its importance as a factor of production, especially its motivational aspects that offered to the common people an incentive to change their present condition and realize a better life—hope! That was certainly the case for many, not everyone, who took advantage of that opportunity and eventually created, and became, the middle class and the backbone and pillars of democracy, controlling the national political process, creating the needed wealth balance, through fiscal policies, taxation, subsidies, transfer programs, the bridge between the extreme classes.

In fact, it is not an exaggeration to state that the sons and daughters of this middle class are in control of the capitalists' corporate wealth; they are their own chief executive officers. Furthermore, the corporations today are not the sole ownership of the rich, but are also the property of the middle class! The problem with the corporate world today is not the Marxian exploitation thesis at work, but the misuse and abuse of power by a "few" CEOs of big corporations, enterprises, and institutions directed at, and affecting, not only the workers but the stockholders and the consumers as well. These are the sons and daughters that came from our middle-class ranks, proving once again that "greed" has no class loyalty, nor social boundaries.

Economics is the study of how we, the people, create wealth by working hard, not only for our survival but also to build a place of safety and security and to continuously improve our human condition, in part directed by man's natural instinct to survive, ordained, as if by natural forces, laws, competition, the selection of the fittest process, the laws of supply and demand, etc., and in perhaps greater part determined and driven by the inner forces of man, his impulsive desire to create and excel, to demonstrate his unique essence as a human being, separate and above the animal kingdom, perhaps a preparation and strive to enter the kingdom of God!

The quest for man's nature and his essence has led to great difficulties in defining our creation, our existence, our purpose, and ourselves. Man, through time, began to rely more and more on his intelligence to reduce these difficulties. He began to imagine, wonder, reason, experiment, discover, organize, and build things, which set him apart from other creatures. At that time, man was on his way to discovering and developing his essence, in conjunction with other men, in a social setting, interacting and interrelating with one another, exerting and applying efforts and energy, not only to survive but to discover, invent, and find answers to the enduring questions. Man is on a quest to solve the riddle of his own creation and destination. Here, his efforts are not compelled by natural forces, but by his own inner impulses and desire to know and discover, and find meaning and joy in that journey! Because of this, we must reject the simplistic view and explanation that man is motivated solely by greed and/or hunger in order to work. His motives are different and vary as he moves along the evolutionary process and progress of civilization: they are economic, they are personal/family, they are political, they are social, and they are religious motives and motivations. It is unfortunate that both capitalists and communists believe in this simplistic, materialistic view of man's motives to exert and apply his physical and mental powers. Survival is no longer an issue and has not been for some time. Greed for the sake of greed is not a satisfactory explanation; man is much more than that—he has a calling, a challenge to discover the unknown, especially himself and his potential. We often disagree on the means and the method of how best to realize this mission—therein lies our problem, our dilemma!

SOURCES

1. The New English Bible, Gospel of John: Acts of the Apostles (New York: Oxford University Press).

2. Toynbee, Arnold, *A Study of History* (London: Oxford University Press, 1972), Parts II-V: VII.

3. Durant, Will, *The Story of Civilization, III: Caesar and Christ* (New York: Simon and Schuster, 1944).

4. Muggeridge, Malcolm, *A Third Testament* (Boston: Little, Brown and Company, 1976).

5. *The Mentor Philosophers: The Ages of: Belief; Adventure; Reason; Enlightenment; Ideology, and Analysis* (New York: New American Library, 1954-56).

6. *Great Ages of Man: A History of the World's Cultures: Ancient Egypt; Classical Greece; Imperial Rome, The Barbarians and Byzantium* (New York: Time-Life Books, 1966).

7. *The Columbia Viking Encyclopedia.*

8. Hexter, J.H. (ed.), *The Traditions of the Western World.*, Vol. 3. Recent period, esp. section on the Nature and Destiny of Man, by Reinhold Niebuhr (Rand McNally & Co, 1971).

9. Dodson, James (ed.), *Readings in Western Civilization* (Hinsdale, Illinois: The Dryden Press Inc., 1972).

10. Stavrianos, L.S., *The Epic of Modern Man: Readings* (Englewood Cliffs, NJ: Prentice-Hall Inc., 1966).

11. Kuniczak, W.S., *The March* (Garden City, NY: Doubleday and Company Inc., 1979).

12. Singer, Isaac B., *The Manor* (New York: Avon Books, The Hearst Corporation).

13. Murchie, Guy, *The Seven Mysteries of Life* (Boston: Houghton Mifflin Company, 1978.)

14. *New Larousse Encyclopedia of Mythology* (Toronto: Prometheus Press, 1968).

15. *US News & World Report*, "Mysteries of Faith—The Prophets," (Special Edition, 2006, Washington, DC).

16. *Time Journal*, Time Canada Ltd., Toronto, Canada, 2003. Vol. 162, No. 25.

17. *Time* Commemorative Issue, "Pope John Paul II, 1920-2005," Canadian Edition, April 11, 2005, Toronto.

18. *Communist Theory—from Marx to Mao* (New York, N.Y., and Stanford, California: Monarch Press Inc., 1961).

19. Saint Thomas Aquinas, *On Being and Essence;* Translated with an Introduction and Notes by Armand Maurer C.S.B., M.A., Ph.D., L.M.S. (The Pontifical Institute of Mediaeval Studies, Toronto, Canada, 1949).

CPSIA information can be obtained at www.ICGtesting.com
Printed in the USA
LVOW13s1638100214

373097LV00034B/1586/P

9 781484 188880